EASY GARDENS

Small Gardens

EASY GARDENS

Small Gardens

Becke Davis

MetroBooks

MetroBooks

An Imprint of the Michael Friedman Publishing Group, Inc.

Library of Congress Cataloging-in-Publication Data

Davis, Becke.
    Small gardens / Becke Davis.
        p.cm.—(Easy gardens)
    Includes bibliographical references (p.) and index.
    ISBN 1-58663-085-7 (alk. paper)
        1. Landscape gardening. 2. Gardening. I. Title. II. Series.

SB473 .D379 2001
635.9—dc

212001044025

Editor: Susan Lauzau
Art Director: Jeff Batzli
Designers: Jennifer Markson and Wendy Fields
Color Illustrations: Susan Kemnitz
Blueprints Illustrations: Jennifer Markson
Photography Editor: Paquita Bass
Production Directors: Richela Fabian Morgan and Michael Vagnetti

Color separations by Bright Arts (Singapore) Pte Ltd
Printed in China by Leefung-Asco Printers Ltd.

1 3 5 7 9 10 8 6 4 2

For bulk purchases and special sales, please contact:
Michael Friedman Publishing Group, Inc.
Attention: Sales Department
230 Fifth Avenue
New York, NY 10001
212/685-6610 FAX 212/685-3916

Visit our website:
www.metrobooks.com

Dedication

To my husband, Marty, and my kids, Jessica and Jonathan, who have come to dread the word "deadline"

To my new sister-in-law, Lisa Davis, and my soon-to-be sister-in-law, Kate Read

To Theresa Regan—in memory of her son, Marty Regan, my neighbor and gardening friend

To Jan Carr, in memory of Chance

And to my parents, Patti and Hank Villars, in honor of their fiftieth wedding anniversary.

Contents

Contents

HOW TO USE THIS BOOK

This book is designed to walk you step by step through the process of planning and planting a beautiful, low-maintenance garden. Ten different theme gardens let you choose the look that suits you best, and each garden plan contains a detailed blueprint plus close-up portraits that describe all the plants featured in the plan. For each garden discussed, you'll find basic "how-to" information on planting, plus a list of necessary tools and equipment. Special boxes give good advice on plant substitutions, garden accents, and other details that might be useful to beginning gardeners, while a "Calendar of Care" points out the necessary maintenance for each season. There are also suggestions for ways to customize these plans to suit your particular landscape needs.

Flip through the pages to familiarize yourself with the plans and plants, then pick a garden plan that you like. Before picking up a spade (or even driving to the garden center), make sure to read "Things You Need to Know" beginning on page 10. This will give you the basics you'll need to get started. Next, read through all the information for the garden plan you've chosen. Some of the questions you have— "How much maintenance is required during the year?" or "How big will this plant grow?"—will be answered as you read. Refer back to Things You Need to Know as you plan and plant; while each garden design section explains the steps you need to take to plan, install, and care for your garden, the general introduction provides information in greater detail about such topics as digging planting holes and proper watering practices.

Note that some of the plans are very straightforward, using only a few types of plants, while others are a bit more involved. Whichever plan you choose, you are only a few simple steps away from a beautiful, healthy garden just outside your window.

THINGS YOU NEED TO KNOW

1. How to Prepare the Planting Area

You should begin by testing your soil to learn whether you need to add any nutrients or whether the pH needs to be adjusted. Home testing kits are widely available at garden centers and nurseries; your county agricultural extension agent can also arrange to have the soil tested for you (look in the government pages of your local telephone book). Many landscape contractors provide this service, as well. With the results of the test will come a prescription for fixing any soil deficiencies.

Next, mark off the area where you want to install the planting bed. Use a narrow, square-ended spade to slice under the sod and lift it up. If you remove the sod in small strips it will be easier to lift. Keep the blade of the spade sharp so you will be digging up as little soil as possible with the sod.

Loosen the soil in the planting bed. This can be done with a small power tiller or by digging with a garden fork or a pointed shovel to a depth of about 8 to 12 inches, moving across the length and width of the bed gradually. Whichever way you choose to loosen the soil, carefully remove weeds and stones by hand. Amendments to soil can be added at this time if needed; among the most common soil amendments are peat moss (never spread this on top of the soil—it will draw water away from plant roots), shredded leaves, sand, aged manure, and compost.

Go around the edges of the bed with the spade, digging a clean, straight edge a few inches deep to separate the bed from the surrounding lawn.

2. Digging the Planting Holes

Years ago the saying was, "Don't dig a five cent hole for a twenty-five cent plant." With the price of trees today, digging a proper hole takes on even greater importance. Loosen the soil down a few feet deeper and wider than the rootball of a tree or shrub. Angle the hole so that it is wider at the top than at the bottom. Mix in some peat moss or aged manure (fresh manure can burn the plant's roots) if you want, but there is some disagreement about the value of amending soil in tree planting holes. Some experts believe that by "spoiling" the tree with amended soil, the roots will resist pushing through the hard subsoil surrounding the hole and wind around themselves in the hole instead. Roots winding around themselves will eventually kill the tree. Put about half of the soil you have dug up back into the hole; save the rest of it in a pile next to the tree (you may want to pile it on black plastic, to protect the lawn).

3. Preparing Trees and Shrubs for Planting

Carry heavy trees or shrubs to the planting area in a wheelbarrow or on a sturdy dolly. Lift the plant with one hand grasping the base of the trunk and the other hand braced on the rootball or container. Never lift a heavy plant by the branches alone, and be careful not to drop it—have helpers on hand, especially if you are working with a tall tree. Cut through any rope or twine that is tied around the base of the plant, and either cut away or fold back any loose burlap. Burlap and twine are made out of biodegradable natural fibers, but today many nurseries are using look-alike products that include synthetic fibers that will never break down. To be safe, cut back any string because it could strangle the plant. Burlap, natural or synthetic, can act like a wick, drawing water away from the root zone, so be sure to either remove it or bury all traces of the burlap below the surface of the soil.

To remove a large plant from a container, lay it on its side and carefully roll the container back and forth to loosen the soil. With one hand on the trunk and one hand on the base of the container, gently pull the plant out of the container. There should not be a tightly packed block of roots, or a lot of roots coming out of the base of the container—these could be signs of a stressed plant. When purchasing plants, avoid those with broken or cracked trunks, diseased-looking leaves, or roots wrapped around the base of the tree.

4. Planting Trees and Shrubs

Place the tree or shrub into the planting hole on top of the loosened soil. You may want a helper to stand back and tell you if the tree or shrub is planted straight. Decide which part of the plant you want to face forward, too, in case one side looks better than another. Once the plant is level, straight, and centered in the hole, start filling in around the sides of the plant, using the soil you have set aside (see number 2). Most plants perform better when planted slightly above the level of the ground; this can

also keep the roots out of standing water in areas where the drainage is slow. Never install plants deeper in the hole than they were planted at the nursery. You can usually see a mark on the trunk to show where the soil level was. Planting so that mark is below the soil can eventually kill the tree or shrub. Once all the soil has been filled in, create a hollow in the soil around the trunk or base of the plant. This will direct water right to the root zone.

5. Initial Pruning

When trees and shrubs are dug at the nursery to be balled and burlapped or put in containers, a good portion of their roots are removed. Some nurseries prune the branches to match the number of roots they have removed; this practice can make transplanting slightly less stressful to the plant. Using pruning shears or lopping shears (for larger branches), remove any branches or twigs that have broken during the planting process. Also look for any crossed branches that may cause problems when they get larger, and for branches that tend to cross over and cut off the trunk. Again, when these branches get larger they could cause problems, so it is best to remove them when they are young.

6. Planting Perennials

Give perennials a good-sized planting hole, about 12 inches deep and wide. As with trees and shrubs, put half of the loosened soil back into the hole and set the rest aside. Perennials in gallon-sized containers usually have pretty well-established roots, and plants this size will help a new garden to look "filled in" much more quickly than if smaller or bareroot plants are used. However, there is nothing wrong with planting small or bareroot plants— they just take a little longer to get started. Remove plants from containers by laying the container on its side and rolling it back and forth gently to loosen the soil and roots. Lift the plant carefully by the base of the stem and set it in the planting hole. Make sure the plant is level and with its best face forward, then carefully fill in the remainder of the soil around the base of the plant. Hollow out the soil around the base of the plant to encourage water to go right to the root zone.

7. Fertilizing: Should I or Shouldn't I?

There are all kinds of fertilizer formulations available, but don't get locked into the idea that you have to continually fertilize to produce healthy plants. Unlike lawns, many shrubs and trees are weakened by over-fertilizing, and fertilizing late in the season can actually make a tree more likely to suffer from winter damage. With annuals and perennials, many fertilizers encourage fast, lush growth of the foliage, but cause smaller and fewer flowers to bloom. Fertilizers can also burn the roots and foliage of plants if incorrectly applied, so use them with caution. If the soil is at the proper pH level for the plant and soil tests show that the necessary nutrients are available in the soil, you may not need to add any additional fertilizer. Remember that fertilizers are supplements—think of them like vitamins, sometimes useful but not always necessary.

8. Planting from Seed

In the garden plans featured in this book, I have generally indicated which annuals are best planted from seed and which are more easily purchased in pots or flats. Where seeds are indicated, they can be planted directly in the soil of the planting area. Use a level-headed rake or a garden fork to make shallow furrows in the soil. Sprinkle the seeds as evenly as possible into the furrows, then use the back of the level-headed rake to smooth the soil back over the top of the seeds. Use a gentle

spray hose attachment to keep the seeds watered regularly—a strong spray could flood the area and wash the seeds away.

Thinning the seedlings can be a painful process for new gardeners, but it's an important one. After the seedlings have come up, pull out about half of them and throw them away. This gives the remaining seedlings their best chance to thrive.

9. Planting Small Bulbs, Annuals, and Groundcovers

Plants in flats and small containers should be removed with extreme care; lift each out gently, grasping the base of its stem. Use a narrow-bladed hand trowel to dig holes for annuals and groundcovers that come in flats. Herbs and other plants that come in small pots should be planted in good-sized holes (about twice as deep and wide as the rooted area) so you may need to use a shovel. Tiny bulbs can be planted easily by making holes with a dibble (a hand implement expressly for making small holes) and dropping the bulbs into the hole. Use a narrow-bladed trowel to cover the holes with soil. Where larger bulbs are indicated in the plans, instructions for planting depths are included.

10. Mulching the Bed

Mulch is a finishing touch that makes a bed look professional and polished. You can purchase it by the bag, which is fine for small planting areas, or by the cubic yard, which is the cheapest way to purchase larger quantities. Use a square-scoop shovel or a narrow-tined pitchfork for lifting and moving mulch; use a level-headed rake for spreading mulch in large areas with shrubs and trees; spread mulch by hand around annuals, perennials, and groundcovers.

11. Watering Your Plants

Water the new transplants carefully over a period of several weeks. Each plant should receive about an inch of water a week in its root zone. Use a soft spray attachment on the hose to prevent the soil from being washed away. If there has not been much rain, place a wooden stick or pencil into the ground to a depth of several inches. If marks on the stick show moisture at a depth of only an inch or two, you will probably want to water more deeply. A deep watering once a week is more beneficial than a light sprinkling of the surface soil day after day. Water early in the day, before the sun is at its peak. Water applied in the afternoon will evaporate quickly.

12. The Difference Between Annuals and Perennials

An annual grows from seed, flowers, and produces seeds all in one year. It then dies and must be replaced unless it is self-seeding, that is, unless it scatters its seeds, which come up the next year. Annuals are often thought of as "cheap and cheerful"; they add color and grow quickly, filling in gaps that might exist in the garden until slower-growing perennials are well-established.

Perennials live more than two years; their roots survive over the winter (unless the plant is grown outside its hardiness zone [see number 13]), and the plant returns year after year. Some perennnials survive indefinitely given the right conditions, while others last only four or five years. There are also biennials, which come to maturity over two seasons and then die (but often reseed), and bulbs, which typically reappear for years before becoming exhausted and dying.

13. Figuring Out Your Plant Hardiness Zone

Plant hardiness zones indicate whether a plant is ideally suited for the average weather conditions in a particular climate. The zones provide guidelines for which plants will survive in which regions, but are not guarantees that a plant will make it through a particularly severe winter or a scorching summer, and the particular conditions in each garden will also affect a plant's performance. Consult the map on page 136 to determine your hardiness zone, and then check the zones listed in the "Getting to Know the Plants" section of the plan you have chosen to make sure that the plants are suited for your area. Most of the plants in these plans have been chosen for their reliability in a wide array of regions.

WHAT YOU WILL NEED

Every gardener should have some basic tools. It's amazing how those tools will multiply, as each spring shiny new implements call out to you from garden center aisles...but that is for the future. For now, start with the essentials. Beginning gardeners may be able to make do with inexpensive tools, but anyone who plans to spend a fair amount of time in the garden will reap the rewards of quality tools. If you have questions about which brand is best or which tool is best for a specific job, don't ask a salesperson—ask a gardener. If you have neighbors who like to garden, you might consider a tool-sharing arrangement to cut down on the purchase of tools you won't need very often.

Digging and Planting Tools

Forks

- A pitchfork, for scooping up mulch
- A garden fork, for breaking up the soil

Spades and Shovels

- A narrow, square-ended spade, for digging straight-sided holes, as well as cutting and lifting sod
- A narrow transplanting spade, for digging among existing plants
- A round-pointed shovel, for digging and lifting soil

Hand Tools

- A broad-bladed trowel, for planting average-sized annuals and perennials
- A narrow-bladed trowel, for installing small transplants, annuals from flats, or smaller bulbs, also useful for planting in containers

Maintenance Tools and Equipment

- A weeding hoe, convenient because it has a hoe on one side and forked hoe for removing weeds on the other, or an old-fashioned garden hoe, for weeding and cultivating the soil

- A level-headed rake, for smoothing and leveling the soil in a new planting area

- Lopping shears, for removing dead branches from trees or shrubs, also for pruning

- Pruning shears—these come in two styles, anvil pruners or bypass pruners, but only one is necessary; both do the job, so choose the one you're most comfortable handling—my personal preference is for the bypass pruner

- A sturdy wheelbarrow, for hauling materials to and from the planting area

- Gardening gloves—leather or heavy rubber gloves are handy when working around thorns, otherwise sturdy canvas will suffice

- A basket, bucket, or cart for hauling tools, plants, and small materials

- Sturdy work boots that will survive lots of mud and water

- Gardener's hand soap—find one you like, because regular hand soaps will never get a gardener's hands clean, no matter how hard you scrub

- A watering can for touch-up watering

- A hose with an adjustable spray attachment, for watering in new transplants

- A trash can or recycling bin for used flats, containers, plant tags, etc.

- A landscape recycling bag or, preferably, a compost bin (or heap) for herbaceous and woody debris

- String or foam-covered wire for staking and tying back plants

- Bamboo poles for staking, when necessary

Optional Tools and Equipment

- A garden hat—recommended, but either you are a hat person or you're not

- An edging tool, to keep the edges of beds neat (a square-edge spade will also do the trick)

- A long-handled bulb planter (these also come as hand tools that are useful for shallow-planted bulbs, but this version is easier on the back for the deeper holes needed by daffodils and tulips; transplanting spades will also do the job)

- A dibble—a small hand tool helpful for planting small bulbs

- A mattock—a hand tool with a long handle and a hoe blade on one side and pick-axe on the other (great for breaking up very hard clay or rocky soil)

- A square-scoop shovel, for moving mulch, sand, compost, or manure

- A dandelion weeder—a sharp-bladed, narrow tool to help dig up and remove the whole root

- A scuffle hoe, useful for working the soil and to get rid of weeds

- A retractable hand rake, a handy gadget sold at flower shows and specialty garden centers—it opens to a full-sized rake or shrinks down to a compact, hand-sized rake, convenient for clearing debris from under shrubs and around flowers

- A lawn rake—necessary for lawn care, but optional for garden care, its main purpose is to remove fallen leaves and debris

- Metal peony hoops, for staking peonies

- Hose guides, to direct hoses away from flowers

- Curved pruning saw, for cutting tree branches

- Electric string trimmer, for cutting back tall grasses or weeds

- Power tiller or cultivator, to help turn over soil in small planting areas

This plan is designed to suit the entry spaces of townhouses, condos, and suburban houses, which typically have entrance sidewalks that create square or rectangular patches of ground perfect for small gardens. While you may not have a piece of land laid out exactly as shown, the plants used can be easily adapted to fit areas that are either long and narrow or square and box-shaped. The design can also be repeated if the entrance walk is very long. All of the plants included can be planted in either spring or autumn.

The plants selected for this garden are pretty hardy, disease-resistant, long-blooming, and easy to maintain, and fare best in sun to part shade. For best results, purchase perennials and vines in 1-gallon containers, and shrubs either balled and burlapped or in 1- to 3-gallon-sized containers. All of the plants and vines indicated are hardy perennials that will come back the following spring.

YOU WILL NEED...

- A square-ended spade if sod has to be removed

- A garden fork to loosen the soil

- A round-pointed shovel for planting the shrub and any gallon-size or larger containers of perennials

- A broad-bladed trowel for planting smaller perennials, if needed, and for planting the Madonna lily bulbs

- A wheelbarrow for moving soil, sod, plants, and debris

- Amendments to soil, if needed or desired: peat moss (never spread this on top of the soil, though, or it will draw water away from the plant roots), shredded leaves, sand, aged manure, or compost, for example

- Mulch, as needed, to spread to a depth of 3 inches around the plants when installed

- Supports for the two vines and string or foam-covered wire, if necessary, to train the vines

- Pruning shears to cut away any dead, diseased, or damaged branches or flowers

- Garden gloves and garden shoes or boots

PLANT LIST

1. Goldflame honeysuckle vine (*Lonicera* x *heckrottii*)

2. Sweet autumn clematis (*Clematis terniflora*, syn. *Clematis maximowicziana*)

3. 'Vera Jameson' sedum (*Sedum* x 'Vera Jameson', syn. *Hylotelephium* x 'Vera Jameson')

4. 'Moonbeam' tickseed (*Coreopsis verticillata* 'Moonbeam')

5. 'Longwood Blue' blue mist shrub (*Caryopteris* x *clandonensis* 'Longwood Blue')

6. 'Stella de Oro' compact daylily (*Hemerocallis* x 'Stella de Oro')

7. Madonna lily (*Lilium candidum*)

8. 'White Swan' coneflower (*Echinacea purpurea* 'White Swan')

9. 'Bridget Bloom' foamy bells (x *Heucherella alba* 'Bridget Bloom')

AN ENTRANCE GARDEN

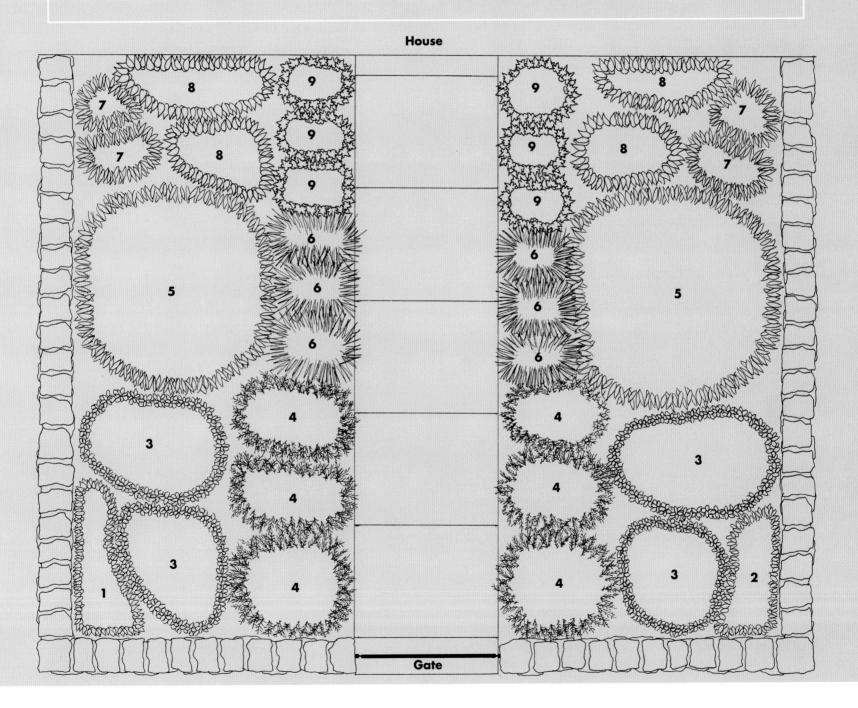

House

Gate

PLANTING THE ENTRANCE GARDEN, STEP BY STEP

Step 1: Get your garden bed ready, following the steps for preparing the planting area on page 10. This garden can be planted in spring or autumn, in sun to part shade.

Step 2: Install the two blue mist shrubs first, making sure that the hole is at least a foot deeper and wider than the shrub's rootball. Prune out broken or diseased branches as they are planted.

Step 3: Next, plant the vines and prune out any broken or diseased branches. Place a trellis (about 6 to 8 feet tall) or other support, such as a tripod, about 6 inches behind the vines. If the vines have long enough tendrils, push the tendrils through the support or trellis; this will encourage the vine to weave through the trellis or support as it climbs. You will need to periodically—about once a week—push new growth through the supports in the same manner. When the vine is established or if you are planting a large-sized vine, you will need to use ties to train the vine up the trellis.

Step 4: Install the plants and bulbs at the back of the border—the 'Vera Jameson' sedum, Madonna lily, and 'White Swan' coneflower—following the plan. Be sure to hollow out the soil around the base of each plant, rather than piling it up where it could rot the plant. Prune out broken or diseased branches as they are planted.

Step 5: Install the plants at the front of the border last—the 'Moonbeam' tickseed, 'Stella de Oro' compact day-lilies, and 'Bridget Bloom' foamy bells. If the border is several feet deep, it may be easiest to spread the mulch at the back of the border before installing the plants at the front. If the difference between the front and back of the border is no longer than the length of a scoop shovel, go ahead and spread the mulch after all the plants have been installed. Hollow out the mulch around the base of the plants, as with the topsoil.

Step 6: Water the new transplants carefully over a period of several weeks. Each plant should receive about an inch of water a week in its root zone. Use a soft spray attachment on the hose to prevent the soil from being washed away. Water early in the day, before the sun is at its peak.

CALENDAR OF CARE

SPRING: *If the garden was planted in autumn, the perennials will show new growth in spring. New foliage will emerge on the shrubs and vines, and the first stalks of the lilies will appear. Apply a slow-release starter (10-10-10 or similar) fertilizer to all plants at this time if you wish. Remove protective mulch from the base of the new transplants, and install new mulch in the planting area to help reduce weed germination. Pull weeds as they emerge. Avoid using herbicides, which can damage or kill newly installed plants.*

SUMMER: *Provide extra support for the vines, if necessary, tying back long or heavy new growth. Continue training new tendrils through the supports. Shear back the 'Moonbeam' tickseed after its first heavy bloom. Remove dead flowers from other perennials as they finish blooming to encourage repeat flowering. Reapply fertilizer about once a month, if desired, but not after about mid-July. Remove weeds regularly and water as needed.*

AUTUMN: *After the first frost, cut back all dead foliage; dispose of undiseased plant waste in a compost heap. Destroy diseased plant remains so they don't contaminate other plants. Prune back the shrubs to improve their shape, if desired. Clean blades of pruners carefully, especially after trimming diseased leaves or branches.*

WINTER: *After the ground has frozen, apply mulch (no more than 3 inches deep) around base of plants to keep roots from heaving out of the soil as the weather goes through freeze and thaw cycles.*

GETTING TO KNOW THE PLANTS

GOLDFLAME HONEYSUCKLE

I. GOLDFLAME HONEYSUCKLE *(Lonicera x heckrotti)*

CLASSIFICATION: Shrubby perennial vine
PLANT HARDINESS ZONES: 5 to 9
ULTIMATE SIZE: To 12' tall
BLOOM TIME: Late spring through late summer
SUN REQUIREMENT: Sun to part shade

Goldflame honeysuckle, a hybrid of the trumpet honeysuckle, can take more shade than many climbers but flowers best in sunny sites with soil that is not allowed to dry out completely. Train it against a trellis or a similar support, pruning back when necessary to keep it in bounds. A perennial vine, this particular honeysuckle does not attract hummingbirds but is less rampant than other forms and has the benefit of fragrant flowers. Aphids, which often afflict honeysuckles, can be easily controlled with insecticidal soaps or sprays, readily available at garden centers.

2. SWEET AUTUMN CLEMATIS

(*Clematis ternifolia*, syn. *C. maximowicziana*, *C. paniculata*, *C. dioscorefolia*)

CLASSIFICATION: Perennial vine
PLANT HARDINESS ZONES: 5 to 9
ULTIMATE SIZE: To 30' tall
BLOOM TIME: Late summer through autumn
SUN REQUIREMENT: Sun to part shade

Sweet autumn clematis is a fast-growing perennial vine that will quickly outgrow a small trellis; it is best suited for a large trellis or an arbor or fence. The flowers are small but fragrant, and cover the vine profusely in late summer. While sweet autumn clematis is adaptable to sun or shade, it flowers best in sun.

SWEET AUTUMN CLEMATIS

'VERA JAMESON' SEDUM

3. 'VERA JAMESON' SEDUM

(*Sedum* x 'Vera Jameson', syn. *Hylotelephium* x 'Vera Jameson', sometimes listed as *Hylotelephium spectabile*)

CLASSIFICATION: Hardy hybrid perennial
PLANT HARDINESS ZONES: 4 to 8
ULTIMATE SIZE: 18"–24" tall and 18" wide
BLOOM TIME: Spring through autumn
SUN REQUIREMENT: Sun to part shade

'Vera Jameson' is distinguished by its succulent, dark purple-bronze foliage, which is tinged with blue and green and accented by colorful flowers. For best results, plant this hardy hybrid perennial in full sun, although it will tolerate partial shade. Cut the plant back in early spring to promote a more compact, heavy flowering habit.

CULTIVAR SUBSTITUTES
You might also try these other recommended sedum hybrids and cultivars:
'Rosy Glow' • 'Sunset Cloud' • 'Meteor' • 'Carmen'
'Strawberries and Cream' • 'Atropurpureum'

'MOONBEAM' TICKSEED

4. 'MOONBEAM' TICKSEED OR THREADLEAF COREOPSIS   (*Coreopsis verticillata* 'Moonbeam')

CLASSIFICATION: Hardy perennial
PLANT HARDINESS ZONES: 4 to 9
ULTIMATE SIZE: 2' tall and wide
BLOOM TIME: Early summer til frost
SUN REQUIREMENT: Sun to part shade

'Moonbeam' tickseed is much admired for its compact habit and soft yellow blossoms, which are ideal for the front of the border. While it fills in to form a low hedge within a year or two, it is not unpleasantly invasive. Heaviest bloom is in early summer, but if you deadhead or shear back the plants, the flowers will continue to bloom until frost. This plant is drought resistant once established (all new transplants need regular watering for at least a few weeks).

5. 'LONGWOOD BLUE' BLUE MIST SHRUB
(*Caryopteris* x *clandonensis* 'Longwood Blue')

CLASSIFICATION: Deciduous shrub
PLANT HARDINESS ZONES: 6 to 9
ULTIMATE SIZE: 4' tall and wide
BLOOM TIME: Mid- to late summer
SUN REQUIREMENT: Full sun

'Longwood Blue' blue mist shrub is somewhat tender, but while it will probably die back to the ground in colder climates (north of Zone 6) during the winter, the roots may survive. Since the flowers form on new growth, the next season's flowers will not be at risk.

COLOR SUBSTITUTES
There are other blue mist shrub cultivars that extend the range of flower colors, including 'Blue Mist', which bears pale blue flowers, and 'Azure', which has bright blue flowers.

COLD-CLIMATE SUBSTITUTE
For gardeners in colder climates who would prefer to substitute a hardier shrub, consider a compact Japanese spirea such as *Spiraea japonica* 'Goldmound', which has gold foliage and pink flowers.

'LONGWOOD BLUE' BLUE MIST SHRUB

'STELLA DE ORO' DAYLILY

6. 'STELLA DE ORO' DAYLILY (*Hemerocallis* x 'Stella de Oro')

CLASSIFICATION: Perennial (sometimes listed as a bulb)
PLANT HARDINESS ZONES: 3 to 9
ULTIMATE SIZE: Less than 2' tall and wide
BLOOM TIME: Early summer to frost
SUN REQUIREMENT: Sun to part shade

This daylily's biggest claims to fame are its dwarf form and its exceptionally long bloom period—expect a heavy bloom in early summer followed by less profuse flowering until frost. This perennial prefers a sunny spot, but does not always hold up well in extreme heat. Southern gardeners might want to plant it where it will have some protection from the afternoon sun. Each daylily flower lives for only one day, but the plant reblooms continuously.

MADONNA LILY

7. MADONNA LILY *(Lilium candidum)*

CLASSIFICATION: Bulb
PLANT HARDINESS ZONES: 5 to 9
ULTIMATE SIZE: To 4' tall
BLOOM TIME: Early summer
SUN REQUIREMENT: Sun, with some protection

With ten to twenty flowers on each stem, the Madonna lily's effect is magnificent even though flowering time is relatively short. Unlike other lilies, the Madonna lily's bulb should be planted no more than 1 inch beneath the soil. Mulch the base of the plant as a winter protection.

8. 'WHITE SWAN' CONEFLOWER

(Echinacea purpurea 'White Swan')

CLASSIFICATION: Perennial
PLANT HARDINESS ZONES: 3 to 9
ULTIMATE SIZE: 2' tall and wide
BLOOM TIME: Midsummer to mid-autumn
SUN REQUIREMENT: Full sun

This hardy perennial has gained fame simultaneously as a foolproof garden flower and as a medicinal herb. The best known forms of coneflower are those with purple blooms, but the white-flowering forms should not be overlooked (in addition to 'White Swan', look for 'White Lustre'). These white forms are more compact than the purple-flowering ones and all perform best in full sun.

'WHITE SWAN' CONEFLOWER

'BRIDGET BLOOM' FOAMY BELLS

9. 'BRIDGET BLOOM' FOAMY BELLS (x *Heucherella alba* 'Bridget Bloom')

CLASSIFICATION: Hardy perennial
PLANT HARDINESS ZONES: 3 to 8
ULTIMATE SIZE: 15"–18" tall and 12"–15" wide
BLOOM TIME: Late spring to mid-autumn
SUN REQUIREMENT: Part shade to sun

This attractive hardy perennial includes the best features of coral bells (*Heuchera* spp.) and foamflowers (*Tiarella* spp.). The foliage is attractive and the plants grow in neatly compact clumps; the flowers are produced prolifically on tall stalks that rise as much as a foot above the foliage. The heaviest bloom is in late spring to early summer; after that flowers will bloom periodically into autumn. Foamy bells performs best in moist soil that is rich in organic matter, in partial shade to sun, and with limited root competition.

A COOL COLOR GARDEN

This garden is designed to offer cooling relief from mid- to late summer, when the heat can be oppressive, and on into autumn. This garden needs to be sited where the plants will be exposed to sun for most of the day (about six hours). If space is at a premium, leave out one of the Russian sages, since they can get quite large.

The Cool Color Garden can be installed in spring for a summer bloom, but there are advantages to planting it in autumn. If you plant in autumn, the roots will have a season to get established before flowering, which can give the plants a good head start. All the plants in this garden are perennials or bulbs, so once you do the work of installation, there will be only routine maintenance and the garden will keep coming back year after year.

YOU WILL NEED...

- A square-ended spade (if sod has to be removed)

- A garden fork to loosen the soil

- A round-pointed shovel for planting any gallon-size or larger containers of perennials

- A broad-bladed hand trowel for planting smaller perennials and for planting the 'Stargazer' lily bulbs

- A wheelbarrow for moving soil, sod, plants, and debris

- Amendments to soil if needed or desired: peat moss (never spread this on top of the soil, or it will draw water away from the plant roots), shredded leaves, sand, aged manure, or compost, for example

- Mulch, as needed, to spread to a depth of 3 inches around the plants when installed

- Pruning shears to cut away any dead, diseased, or damaged branches or flowers

- Garden gloves and garden shoes or boots

PLANT LIST

1. Russian sage (*Perovskia atriplicifolia*)

2. 'Snowbank' starflower (*Boltonia asteroides* 'Snowbank')

3. 'Alma Potschke' New England aster (*Aster novae-angliae* 'Alma Potschke')

4. 'Kobold' spike gayfeather (*Liatris spicata* 'Kobold')

5. 'Stargazer' hybrid lily (*Lilium* x 'Stargazer')

6. Purple coneflower (*Echinacea purpurea*)

7. 'Butterfly Blue' pincushion flower (*Scabiosa columbaria* 'Butterfly Blue')

8. 'Palace Purple' coral bells (*Heuchera micrantha* 'Palace Purple')

A COOL COLOR GARDEN

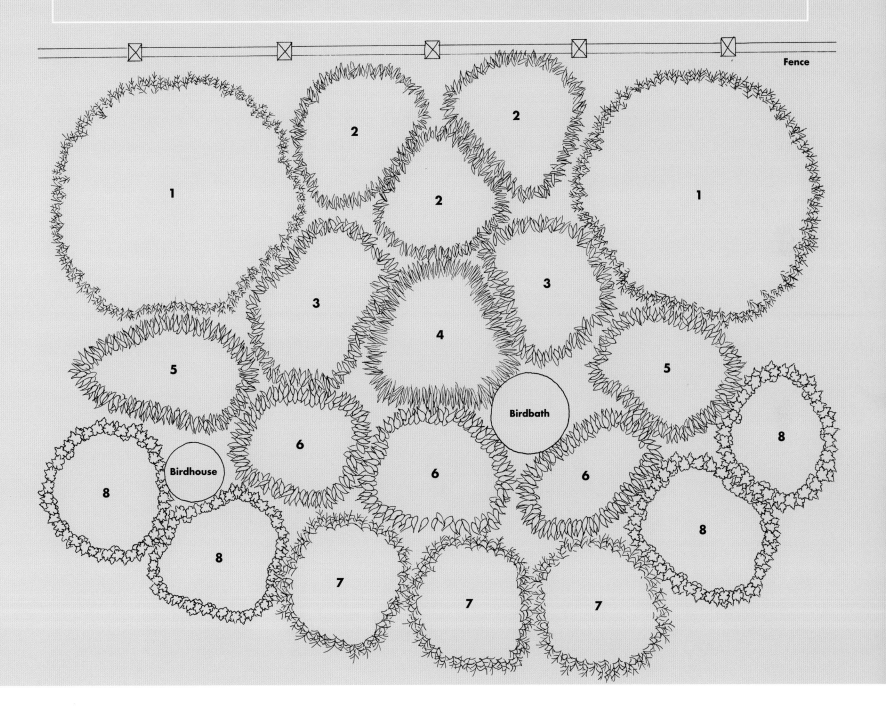

Fence

Birdbath

Birdhouse

PLANTING THE COOL COLOR GARDEN, STEP BY STEP

Step 1: Prepare the planting bed, following the steps on page 10.

Step 2: Plant the 'Stargazer' lily bulbs about 8 inches deep (consult pages 11–14 on digging planting holes and planting bulbs, if you need to review). The flatter part of the bulb should face down; the more pointed end should face up. If the bulbs were packed in excelsior-like material, be sure to remove all of the material before planting. Place a

GOOD ACCENTS FOR THIS GARDEN

Most gardens benefit from an ornament set in among the plants to act as a focal point or to create a sense of surprise when the visitor sees the accent nestled among the leaves and flowers. Consider one of the following accents for this pastel cottage space.

- A birdbath
- A painted watering can
- A piece of garden furniture
- A large garden pot

marker (such as a stick or a golf tee) near the bulbs so you don't disturb them when installing the other plants.

Step 3: Plant the back of the border plants first—the Russian sage and the 'Snowbank' starflowers—and spread mulch around these, forming a hollow near the base of each plant. Prune away broken or diseased foliage and flowers as you install each plant, removing the debris from the planting area. Be sure to remove any weeds or stones you may find in the soil.

Step 4: Next, install the plants intended for the middle of the border—the 'Alma Potschke' New England asters, 'Kobold' spike gayfeather, and purple coneflowers—pruning broken foliage and flowers and applying mulch as in Step 3.

Step 5: Plant the front-of-the-border plants—the 'Butterfly Blue' pincushion flower and the 'Palace Purple' coral bells, pruning and mulching as with the other plants.

Step 6: After planting, water with a gentle spray until the ground is saturated but the plants are not sitting in water. Water the new transplants carefully over a period of several weeks. Each plant should receive about an inch of water a week in its root zone (see "Things You Need to Know" on page 15 for more information on good watering practices).

CALENDAR OF CARE

SPRING: *If you planted your garden in autumn, the perennials will show new growth in spring. By late spring, the first stalks of the lilies will appear. Apply a slow-release fertilizer at this time if you wish. Remove protective mulch from the base of the new transplants, and install new mulch in the planting area to help cut down on weeds. Pull weeds as they emerge. Avoid using herbicides, which can damage or kill the newly installed plants.*

SUMMER: *Pinch back the foliage of the starflowers and the asters to promote a dense growth habit. Remove the dead flowers from other perennials as they finish blooming to encourage repeat flowering. Reapply fertilizer if desired, but not after about mid-July. Remove weeds regularly and water as needed.*

AUTUMN: *After the first frost, cut back all dead foliage; dispose of undiseased plant waste in a compost heap. Destroy diseased plant remains so they don't contaminate other plants. Prune back the Russian sage, if desired, or wait until spring. Clean the blades of pruning shears carefully, especially after trimming diseased leaves or branches. Clean all tools and equipment carefully before storing for the winter.*

WINTER: *After the ground has frozen, apply additional mulch (no more than 3 inches deep) to keep plant roots from heaving out of the soil as the weather goes through freeze and thaw cycles.*

GETTING TO KNOW THE PLANTS

RUSSIAN SAGE

1. RUSSIAN SAGE   (*Perovskia atriplicifolia*)

CLASSIFICATION: Shrubby perennial
PLANT HARDINESS ZONES: 4 to 9
ULTIMATE SIZE: 3'–5' tall and wide
BLOOM TIME: Midsummer to frost
SUN REQUIREMENT: Full sun

This is a great, carefree plant, with flowers variously described as blue, light blue, violet, or lavender blue. The crushed foliage is aromatic, with a scent similar to sage. A fuller plant will result if you cut back the foliage either in late autumn or early spring. Plant in full sun in average to dry soil for best results.

2. 'SNOWBANK' STARFLOWER
(*Boltonia asteroides* 'Snowbank')

CLASSIFICATION: Perennial
PLANT HARDINESS ZONES: 4 to 9
ULTIMATE SIZE: 4' tall and 3' wide
BLOOM TIME: Late summer to autumn
SUN REQUIREMENT: Sun to part shade

The foliage of starflower is neat, but the plant looks uninspiring until the profuse white, daisylike flowers bloom in late summer. Often sturdy enough to remain upright without staking, it can be grown against a fence when staking is needed. To reduce the need for staking, create a shorter, shrubbier plant by cutting back the foliage in late spring or early summer. Plant in full sun in soil that is kept evenly moist. The cultivar 'Snowbank' recommended here is superior to the species and is readily available.

'SNOWBANK' STARFLOWER

3. 'ALMA POTSCHKE' NEW ENGLAND ASTER

(*Aster novae-angliae* 'Alma Potschke')

CLASSIFICATION: Perennial
PLANT HARDINESS ZONES: 4 to 9
ULTIMATE SIZE: To 4' tall and wide
BLOOM TIME: Late summer to frost
SUN REQUIREMENT: Sun to part shade

When you see the vivid pink flowers of the 'Alma Potschke' New England aster in full bloom, it's hard for anything else to compete. 'Alma Potschke' is particularly long-blooming and heavy-blooming, and the brightly colored flowers act as a foil for many other late-blooming plants. Even though this is one of the taller asters, staking is usually not necessary. Pinch back the stems in late spring to promote bushier, more compact growth. For best results, plant in average soil in full sun to part shade.

'ALMA POTSCHKE' NEW ENGLAND ASTER

'KOBOLD' SPIKE GAYFEATHER

4. 'KOBOLD' SPIKE GAYFEATHER, BLAZING STAR

(*Liatris spicata* 'Kobold')

CLASSIFICATION: Perennial
PLANT HARDINESS ZONES: 3 to 9
ULTIMATE SIZE: 3' tall and 2' wide
BLOOM TIME: Mid- to late summer
SUN REQUIREMENT: Full sun

This native plant is very easy to grow as long as it gets full sun; make sure the soil is well-drained, though, because spike gayfeather does not like to have "wet feet" in the winter months. 'Kobold' has brilliant spikes of rosy purple-pink and is low maintenance—it is pest resistant, drought tolerant, and does not require division or staking. It is sometimes listed as a bulb because it grows from corms (you can also start it from seed). An extra benefit—butterflies love it!

COLOR SUBSTITUTES
Other excellent spike gayfeather cultivars include the white-flowering 'Floristan White' and 'Silver Tip', which has lavender flowers.

'STARGAZER' HYBRID LILY

5. 'STARGAZER' HYBRID LILY   (*Lilium* x 'Stargazer')

CLASSIFICATION: Bulb
PLANT HARDINESS ZONES: 5 to 8
ULTIMATE SIZE: To 36" tall
BLOOM TIME: Mid- to late summer
SUN REQUIREMENT: Full sun to part shade

'Stargazer' is stunning in a garden setting, where its highly fragrant flowers announce its presence long before the blossoms come into view. Apply a "bulb booster" fertilizer in early spring; other than that, little maintenance is necessary. In very cold climates, cut back the stalks and mulch over the bulbs to protect them from damaging freeze and thaw conditions.

6. PURPLE CONEFLOWER   (*Echinacea purpurea*)

CLASSIFICATION: Perennial
PLANT HARDINESS ZONES: 3 to 10
ULTIMATE SIZE: 3' tall and wide
BLOOM TIME: Midsummer to early autumn
SUN REQUIREMENT: Full sun

Purple coneflowers are undemanding and easy to grow in a variety of conditions: they are drought tolerant, do not need staking, and are attractive to birds and butterflies. The daisy-type flowers have dark cones and petals, or rays, that droop from the cone. Flower color varies slightly from rosy pink to purple, but the differences are not prominent. Plant in full sun in average soil; deadhead for a later repeat bloom or leave the seedheads if you want to attract birds.

CULTIVAR SUBSTITUTES
Other excellent coneflower cultivars include:
'Magnus' • 'Bright Star' • 'Crimson Star' • 'Bravado' • 'Robert Bloom'

PURPLE CONEFLOWER

7. 'BUTTERFLY BLUE' PINCUSHION FLOWER, SCABIOUS

(*Scabiosa columbaria* 'Butterfly Blue')

CLASSIFICATION: Perennial
PLANT HARDINESS ZONES: 4 to 7
ULTIMATE SIZE: 18"–24" tall and wide
BLOOM TIME: Summer to autumn
SUN REQUIREMENT: Sun to part shade

'Butterfly Blue' has much more to offer than older pincushion flower varieties: it is compact and very long blooming, with flowers that blend well with other plants and seem to glow in the dusk. Deadheading will increase and prolong the bloom period. In very hot climates, plant pincushion flower in part shade, otherwise full sun is fine. This is a fairly undemanding plant but it does require well-drained soil; it will perform best in soil that is rich in organic matter.

'BUTTERFLY BLUE' PINCUSHION FLOWER

'PALACE PURPLE' CORAL BELLS

8. 'PALACE PURPLE' CORAL BELLS

(*Heuchera micrantha* 'Palace Purple')

CLASSIFICATION: Perennial
PLANT HARDINESS ZONES: 4 to 9
ULTIMATE SIZE: Approximately 30" tall and 24" wide
BLOOM TIME: Early to midsummer
SUN REQUIREMENT: Sun to part shade

Although the flowers of this plant are attractive, some feel that they detract from the foliage that is its claim to fame. The neat, mounding form makes it an ideal plant for the front of the border, and it requires little maintenance to keep it looking good. Like other forms of coral bells, 'Palace Purple' will perform best in either full sun or part shade, in spots where the soil is rich in organic matter and moist but well-drained (note that where the sun is very strong, the foliage color can fade somewhat).

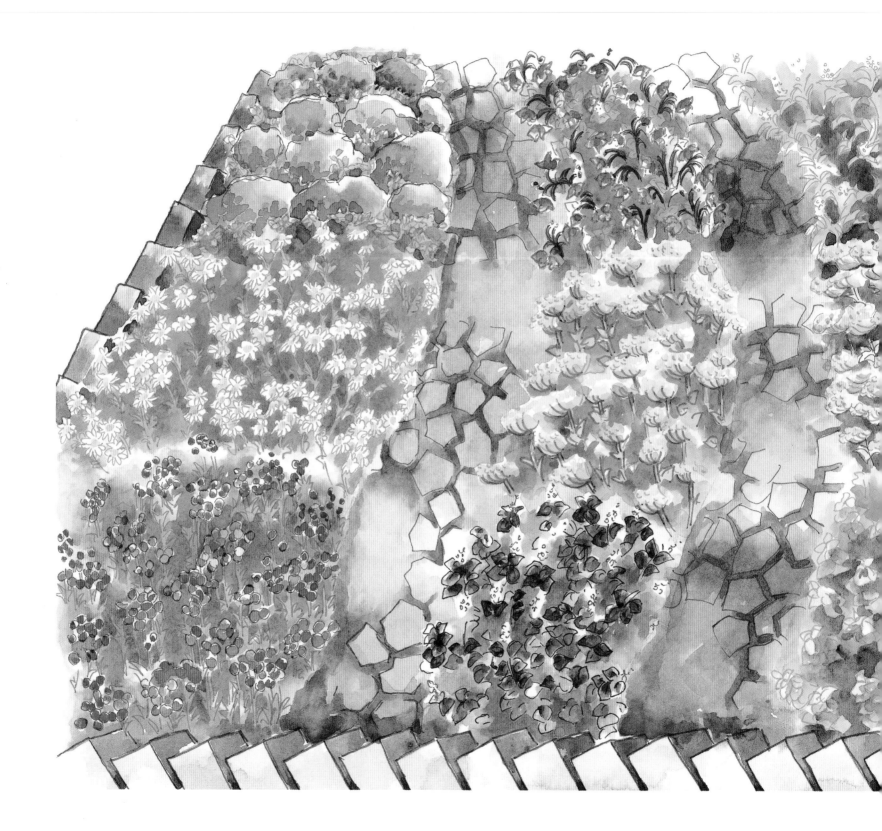

A RAISED BED HERB GARDEN

You don't have to be a gourmet cook to enjoy an herb garden, but handling the herbs and inhaling their wonderful fragrances might just encourage you to take up the culinary arts. This garden plan features a sampling of popular herbs in a very straightforward design. The raised bed makes the herbs more accessible and contains the roots of the more invasive species. Details on raised beds and berms can be found in a sidebar on page 46. If you'd rather not install a raised bed or simply don't have the space, the same plants can be planted in containers and set in a sunny area on a deck or patio.

Plant this garden in spring, after the danger of frost has passed. A number of the herbs in this plan are hardy and will survive the winter; expect the rest to be wiped out by the first hard frost. Whether you start the herbs in this design from seed in early spring or purchase small pots of the herbs to plant in late spring, they will be useful and attractive for most of the summer and into the autumn.

YOU WILL NEED...

- Materials to build a raised bed or topsoil to berm up the grade of the soil

- Topsoil, as needed, to fill the raised bed or build a berm

- A scoop shovel to move the soil

- A level-headed rake for smoothing the soil

- A narrow-bladed hand trowel for planting the herbs

- A wheelbarrow for moving soil, plants, and debris

- Amendments to soil if needed or desired: peat moss, shredded leaves, sand, aged manure, or compost, for example

- Mulch, as needed, to spread to a depth of 3 inches around the plants when installed*

- Small hand trimmers or scissors to clip herbs

- Garden gloves

*Some gardeners prefer to cultivate around herbs with a hoe or hand fork, rather than mulching; if you go this route, do mulch over the planting area for winter protection.

PLANT LIST

1. Creeping thyme (*Thymus serpyllum*)

2. Borage (*Borago officinalis*)

3. French tarragon (*Artemisia dranunculus*)

4. Oregano (*Origanum vulgare*)

5. Roman chamomile (*Chamaemelum nobile*)

6. Dill (*Anethum graveolens*)

7. Bronze fennel (*Foeniculum vulgare* 'Purpurascens')

8. Hyssop (*Hyssopus officinalis*)

9. Chives (*Allium schoenoprasum*)

10. 'Dark Opal' basil (*Ocimum basilicum* 'Dark Opal')

11. Sweet basil (*Ocimum basilicum*)

12. Common garden thyme (*Thymus vulgaris*)

A RAISED BED HERB GARDEN

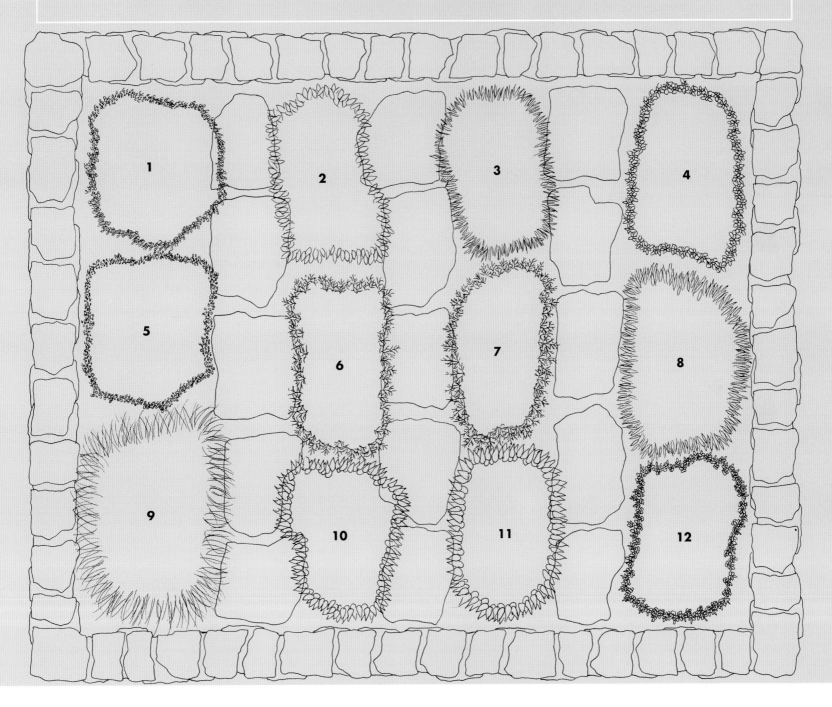

PLANTING THE RAISED BED HERB GARDEN, STEP BY STEP

Step 1: Prepare the berm or planting bed to your personal specifications. See the sidebar at right for details on options.

Step 2: Add topsoil and amendments to raise the berm or fill the raised bed. Do not overfill the raised bed, or the excess soil will wash away when it rains or when you water the plants.

Step 3: Following the steps on page 14 for planting small bulbs, annuals, and groundcovers, plant each herb in order of its appearance on the garden plan. Plants purchased in containers can be installed in the planting bed as soon as the frost date is past. You may mulch herbs as you would any other perennial or annual, but some gardeners prefer to leave herb gardens mulch-free, keeping the weeds out the old-fashioned way—with a hand fork and a hoe.

Step 4: Water the new transplants and seedlings carefully over a period of several weeks. Each plant should receive about an inch of water a week in its root zone.

Use a soft spray attachment on the hose to prevent the soil from being washed away. Water early in the day, before the sun is at its peak.

BERMS AND RAISED BEDS

There are many benefits to gardening in a raised bed. If you have poor or heavily compacted soil, unworkable clay, or excessively sandy soil, you can add your own amended soil by building a raised bed. Easy-to-use kits for constructing a raised bed of about 6 to 8 inches in height are on the market, but you can also use large stones or landscape timbers to retain the soil in a raised garden bed.

A berm is slightly different from a raised bed, although it can be used the same way. Create a berm by adding soil to raise the grade by 6 to 12 inches. Any more than that and you will need a retaining wall to support the soil; even a 12-inch berm should only be that deep in the center, with the sides gradually sloping down. Berms can be used to create island beds, crescent shaped beds, or any sort of defined shape raised above the level grade of the landscape. Berms add interest by changing the grade and, like raised beds, give gardeners the opportunity to bring in soil that is to their own specifications.

CALENDAR OF CARE

SPRING: *Install plants and seedlings as detailed. Keep weeds out of the bed, but do not use herbicides, especially with plants that will be eaten.*

SUMMER: *Take clippings of herbs for kitchen use on a regular basis. This keeps the plants dense and compact,*

STARTING HERBS FROM SEED

If you choose to start herbs from seed, you may want to use seed trays that have been designed for mistake-free planting; or you could use peat pots designed to be soaked in water before planting. Plant seeds to the depth indicated on the seed packet. Do not allow peat pots or planting soil to dry out. Thin out excess seedlings after germination. Prepare seedlings with at least two leaves for the outdoors by setting them out for a few hours each day prior to planting, bringing them back in at night. After two to three days it will be safe to plant them outdoors. Peat pots can be planted directly into the garden bed once seedlings have about three to four sets of leaves and after the last frost date. Do not fertilize young seedlings.

and it's great for improving recipes, too! (Many herbs are most flavorful just prior to flowering.) Remove dead flower heads from chives and shear or clip the chamomile to keep it neat-looking. Support the fennel and dill with stakes if necessary.

AUTUMN: *After the first frost, cut back all dead foliage; dispose of undiseased plant waste in a compost heap. Destroy diseased plant remains so they don't contaminate other plants. Prune back perennial herbs such as thyme and oregano to improve their shape, if desired. Herbs can also be dug up in autumn and transferred into containers, to be overwintered indoors. Replant in the bed or berm in spring, after re-acclimatizing plants to the weather by placing them outdoors during the day and bringing them in at night for a few days.*

WINTER: *After the ground has frozen, apply additional mulch (no more than 3 inches deep) to keep perennial plant roots from heaving out of the soil as the weather goes through freeze and thaw cycles.*

GETTING TO KNOW THE PLANTS

CREEPING THYME

1. CREEPING THYME   (*Thymus serpyllum*)

CLASSIFICATION: Perennial herb
PLANT HARDINESS ZONES: 5 to 9
ULTIMATE SIZE: Spreading groundcover 8"–18" tall
BLOOM TIME: Late spring to late summer
SUN REQUIREMENTS: Full sun

Creeping thyme is a very dense, low-growing herb that can be used as a groundcover, as a rock garden plant, or to edge a perennial bed. Since it can take a certain amount of foot traffic, it is often planted between paving stones on paths and patios. The foliage is very fragrant when stepped on, crushed, or brushed against. Plant creeping thyme in a sunny site with well-drained soil and clip it as often as you like. Clippings can be used for flavoring or garnish, or dried for use in potpourri. Bees love thyme, along with many other herbs, so do not plant it near children's play areas.

2. BORAGE   (*Borago officinalis*)

CLASSIFICATION: Annual herb
PLANT HARDINESS ZONES: 7 to 9
ULTIMATE SIZE: To 3' tall and wide
BLOOM TIME: Late spring to late summer
SUN REQUIREMENT: Full sun

Borage is a large, sprawling plant with hairy foliage and masses of tiny, drooping, blue flowers. Although borage does have medicinal uses, it does not dry well and is best known for its edible flowers and leaves. The freshly picked flowerheads can be used to decorate cakes or as an accent in fruit salads (note that eating borage in large amounts or over a long period can be dangerous). Although borage is an annual, it self-seeds freely. When planting a new herb garden, set out borage seeds in early spring. Young plants may be purchased but they don't always transplant well. Full-grown plants may need to be staked to keep them from getting floppy. Borage is very attractive to bees.

BORAGE

3. FRENCH TARRAGON, TARRAGON

(Artemisia dranunculus)

CLASSIFICATION: Perennial herb
PLANT HARDINESS ZONES: 4 to 8
ULTIMATE SIZE: To 3' tall and wide
BLOOM TIME: Midsummer through autumn
SUN REQUIREMENT: Full sun

French tarragon is a highly aromatic herb with many culinary uses; it is best when used fresh but can be dried or frozen for winter use. The foliage is attractive and aromatic, with a strong but savory flavor; use fresh tarragon sparingly in salad dressings and sauces for fish, including tartar sauce; use larger leaves to make tarragon vinegar. Plant French tarragon in a sunny, very well-drained site, giving the roots a lot of room to spread. Cut back the foliage in winter and cover the roots with straw or mulch. Tarragon may cause health problems if eaten in very large quantities or over an extended period of time.

FRENCH TARRAGON

OREGANO

4. OREGANO, WILD MARJORAM *(Origanum vulgare)*

CLASSIFICATION: Perennial herb
PLANT HARDINESS ZONES: 5 to 9
ULTIMATE SIZE: To 3' tall, spreading
BLOOM TIME: From early summer to mid-autumn
SUN REQUIREMENT: Full sun

The aromatic foliage of oregano, or wild marjoram, is highly flavored, making it a popular addition to pizza and spaghetti sauces, and as a seasoning for fish or meat. The roots of this herb spread rapidly and can become invasive; this tendency can be controlled for the most part by growing the plant in a large coffee container and then burying the whole container in the planting bed. Pinch as needed for culinary use, but note that the leaves are said to be sweetest just before flowering. Plant in full sun in very well-drained soil. While oregano will grow in shade, both flowers and fragrance are better in full sun. It is very attractive to bees.

ROMAN CHAMOMILE

5. ROMAN CHAMOMILE
(*Chamaemelum nobile*, syn. *Anthemis nobilis*)

CLASSIFICATION: Perennial herb
PLANT HARDINESS ZONES: 4 to 9
ULTIMATE SIZE: Low spreading groundcover, up to 12" tall
BLOOM TIME: Midsummer to early autumn
SUN REQUIREMENT: Full sun

Chamomile has long been valued for its medicinal uses; chamomile tea, in particular, is said to soothe indigestion. The profuse, tiny flowers are fragrant, smelling slightly like apples. Established plants can take a certain amount of foot traffic without incurring damage; it can be sheared or mowed, but is best planted between stones or in limited spaces rather than as a replacement for turfgrass. There are many types of chamomile, but this species, Roman chamomile, is said to produce a superior tea. Roman chamomile is drought-tolerant and prefers a site in full sun.

6. DILL   (*Anethum graveolens*)

CLASSIFICATION: Annual herb
PLANT HARDINESS ZONES: 7 to 9
ULTIMATE SIZE: To 3' tall and 2' wide
BLOOM TIME: Mid- to late summer
SUN REQUIREMENT: Full sun

Young dill plants do not usually transplant well, so it is best to plant dill seeds directly into the planting bed in spring, once danger of frost is past. The stalks are tall with feathery, aromatic foliage, and will probably need staking before the plants reach 2 feet in height. Both dill leaves and dill seeds are used as culinary accents—the leaves can be picked at any time but the seeds will not appear until after the flowers finish blooming. When cutting dill to freeze or dry, cut the entire stalk and store it with the leaves still attached (the flavor is best before it flowers).

DILL

7. BRONZE FENNEL   (*Foeniculum vulgare* 'Purpurascens', syn. 'Rubrum')

CLASSIFICATION: Perennial herb
PLANT HARDINESS ZONES: 6 to 9
ULTIMATE SIZE: To 6' tall and 3' wide
BLOOM TIME: Midsummer to early autumn
SUN REQUIREMENT: Full sun

While fennel is regularly used in culinary herb gardens, bronze fennel is so ornamental that it is frequently found in perennial gardens, too. The foliage is a rich purple-pink, copper, bronze, or bronze-green, and creates a stunning background for lower-growing herbs. Fennel has a flavor like licorice; its seeds, roots, shoots and stalks have been used for over a thousand years as a seasoning as well as for medicinal purposes. Fennel can be started from seed indoors, or the seeds can be sown directly into the planting bed after the danger of frost is past.

BRONZE FENNEL

HYSSOP

8. HYSSOP   (*Hyssopus officinalis*)

CLASSIFICATION: Shrubby perennial herb
PLANT HARDINESS ZONES: 3 to 9
ULTIMATE SIZE: To 3' tall, can be sheared to a low hedge
BLOOM TIME: Midsummer to late autumn
SUN REQUIREMENT: Full sun

Hyssop is a woody, aromatic perennial herb that can be trimmed into a low hedge; in warmer regions the foliage is evergreen. The flowers are not prominent but they are long-blooming, and blue flowers are a plus in any garden. The flowers are also attractive to bees and butterflies. Over the centuries hyssop has been used as a flavoring in savories and liqueurs, to make tea and wine, for religious and medicinal purposes, and as an antiseptic cleanser. It can also be dried for use in mixed herbal potpourris. Because hyssop can survive being pruned severely, it is often used as an edging plant in traditional herb knot gardens and in container plantings.

CHIVES

9. CHIVES   (*Allium schoenoprasum*)

CLASSIFICATION: Perennial herb
PLANT HARDINESS ZONES: 6 to 9
ULTIMATE SIZE: To about 2' tall and wide
BLOOM TIME: Spring to midsummer
SUN REQUIREMENT: Sun to part shade

All it takes is one pinch of the slender, grassy, hollow foliage to be reminded that chives are in the onion family. The distinctive flavor is perfect in sauces and soups, and as a garnish for everything from steak to baked potatoes. The pink-purple flowers are very ornamental and the compact clumps of foliage look nice at the front of a border even when the plants aren't in flower. Clip the foliage at any time for culinary use; the flavor is best just before flowering. Take cuttings frequently but do not cut large sections all at once—although chives are relatively hardy, they will not survive drastic pruning.

10. 'DARK OPAL' BASIL   (*Ocimum basilicum* 'Dark Opal')

CLASSIFICATION: Annual herb
PLANT HARDINESS ZONES: 9 to 10
ULTIMATE SIZE: To about 2' tall and wide
BLOOM TIME: Midsummer to early autumn
SUN REQUIREMENT: Full sun

Basils are valuable additions to any herb garden, even though they require a little extra care and protection because they are annuals. 'Dark Opal' is a beautiful purple cultivar of sweet basil; it not only stands out in the herb garden but also adds color to sauces and vinegars. Plant 'Dark Opal' basil in the same way that you would a sweet basil (see the plant portrait for sweet basil).

SUBSTITUTES
Other excellent basils include:
Spicy globe basil (*Ocimum basilicum* 'Spicy Globe') • Lemon basil (*O. citriodorum*) • Holy basil (*O. tenuiflorum*, syn. *O. sanctum*) • Thai basil (*O. americanum* syn. *O. canum*) • Cinnamon basil (*O. basilicum* 'Cinnamon') • Bush basil (*O. basilicum* 'Minimum') • Lettuce leaf basil (*O. basilicum* var. *crispum*) • Ruffled leaf cultivars (*O. basilicum* 'Green Ruffles' and 'Purple Ruffles')

'DARK OPAL' BASIL

11. SWEET BASIL (*Ocimum basilicum*)

CLASSIFICATION: Annual herb
PLANT HARDINESS ZONES: 9 to 10
ULTIMATE SIZE: To about 2' tall and wide
BLOOM TIME: Midsummer to early autumn
SUN REQUIREMENT: Full sun

Sweet basil has wonderfully fragrant foliage. The large, shiny leaves are much more ornamental than the insignificant flowers. To promote better leaf growth, pinch leaves regularly, remove the flowers before they have a chance to form, and keep the plant well watered. The primary ingredient in pesto sauce, basil is also used in vinegar and many tomato dishes. Basil is a tender plant that can be started indoors from seed and transplanted outdoors (in a sunny, sheltered spot) when the plant has several leaflets and when all danger of frost is past.

SWEET BASIL

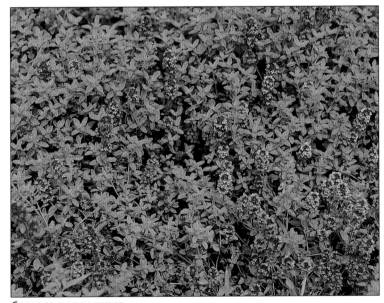

COMMON GARDEN THYME

12. COMMON GARDEN THYME
(*Thymus vulgaris*)

CLASSIFICATION: Shrubby perennial herb
PLANT HARDINESS ZONES: 6 to 9
ULTIMATE SIZE: From 6"–15" tall, shrubby and spreading
BLOOM TIME: Spring to late summer
SUN REQUIREMENT: Full sun

Common thyme is an essential plant for any culinary herb garden; it has also been hailed for centuries as a medicinal herb. The strong fragrance makes it an ideal choice for potpourri; dried thyme is also popular for use in "sleep pillows." Unlike some other thymes, the seeds can be sown directly into the planting bed. Because of its dense, shrubby form, common thyme can be easily pruned into a low hedge or edging plant and is often used in old-fashioned herbal knot gardens.

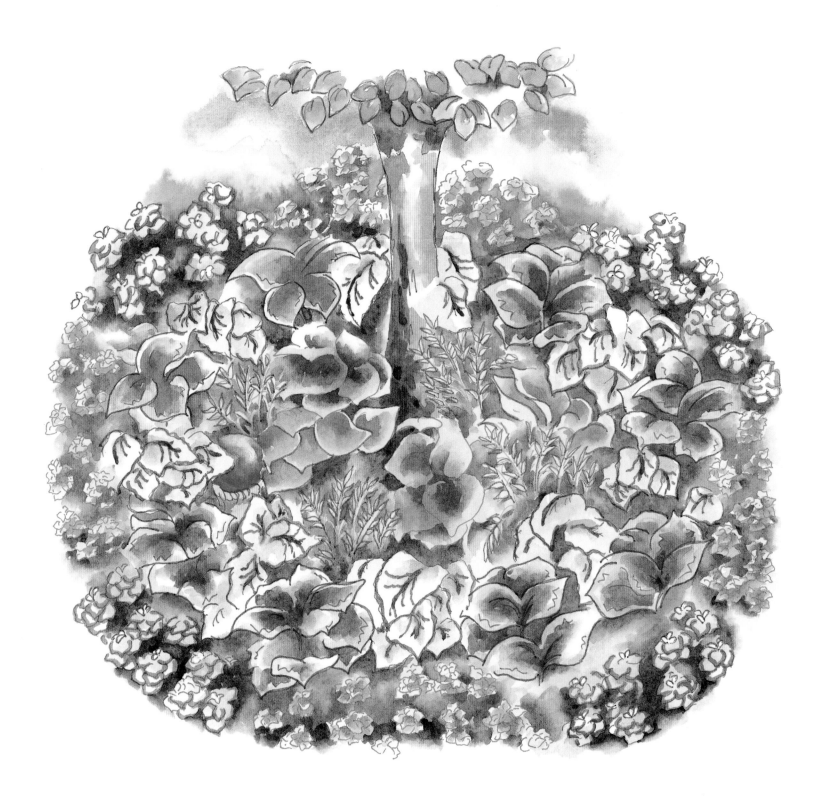

A SHADY TREE CIRCLE

Tree circle plantings are very easy to install and to maintain. The chief concern is getting the new plants into the dirt without damaging the roots of the tree and without changing the grade of the soil around the tree roots by more than an inch or two. A tree circle can be as small as 3 feet in diameter around a young tree or as large as 12 feet in diameter around a mature tree or a stand of tall, upright trees. This plan is based around a large shade tree, but all of the plants shown will also thrive in partial shade.

This garden can be planted in early spring or in autumn (with the exception of the caladiums, which must be planted in spring, since they are not winter hardy). Autumn plantings have an advantage in that they have the time to become at least partly established before they come into foliage and flower. If you plant in autumn, though, be sure to water the transplants regularly and mulch to protect the roots from freeze-and-thaw conditions in winter.

To keep costs down, purchase the hostas, ferns, and caladiums by mail order; you will most likely receive a package of roots packed in something like excelsior—remove the packing and plant the roots into the garden (soaking the roots first, if the mail-order nursery so advises). The hostas, ferns, Japanese spurge, and dead nettle can be purchased and planted in the autumn, but the tender caladiums should be purchased and planted in spring (or you may choose an alternate plant, as described on page 62).

YOU WILL NEED...

- A square-ended spade if sod has to be removed

- A narrow-tined fork to loosen the soil without cutting into tree roots

- A narrow transplanting spade for installing the hostas

- A narrow-bladed hand trowel for installing the smaller plants

- A wheelbarrow for moving soil, sod, plants, and debris

- Amendments to soil if needed or desired: peat moss, shredded leaves, sand, aged manure, or compost, for example

- Mulch, as needed, to spread to a depth of 1–2 inches around the plants when installed

- Small hand clippers or scissors to cut back damaged foliage when planting

- Garden gloves and garden shoes or boots

- A kneeling pad

PLANT LIST

1. 'Sum and Substance' hosta (*Hosta* x 'Sum and Substance')

2. 'Elegans' hosta (*Hosta* x 'Elegans')

3. Male fern (*Dryopteris filix-mas*)

4. 'White Christmas' caladium (*Caladium* x 'White Christmas')

5. 'Francée' hosta (*Hosta* x 'Francée')

6. 'White Nancy' dead nettle (*Lamium maculatum* 'White Nancy')

7. Japanese spurge (*Pachysandra terminalis*)

A SHADY TREE GARDEN

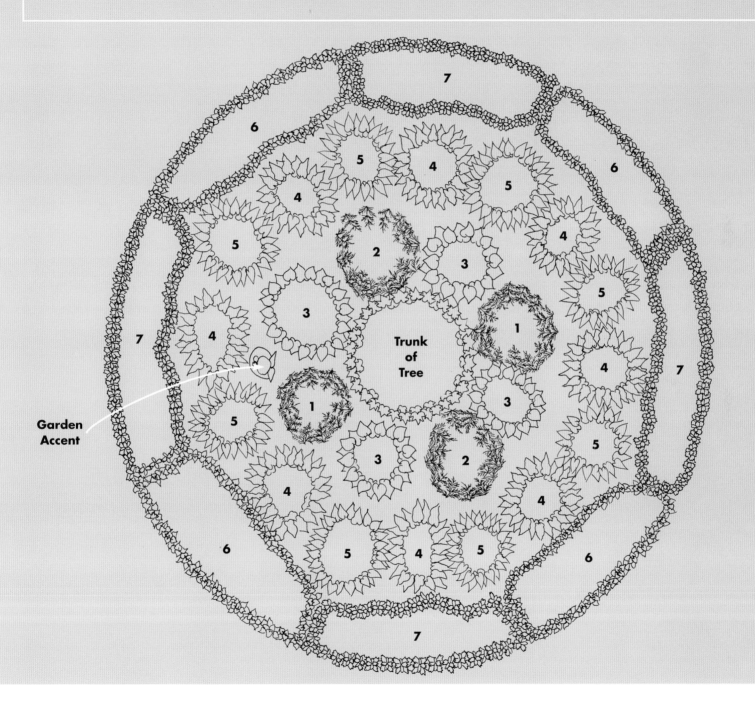

7

6

5 4

4 5

5

2

3

3

6

4

4

7

3 1

Trunk
of
Tree

4

5

Garden
Accent

1

3

5

3 2

5

4

4

7

6 5 4 5 6

7

PLANTING THE SHADY TREE CIRCLE, STEP BY STEP

Step 1: Follow the steps on page 10 that deal with preparing the planting area, taking care not to disturb the tree roots. After removing the sod, loosen the topsoil carefully with a garden fork, then add 2 to 3 inches of topsoil, mixed with amendments if desired.

Step 2: Use a narrow-bladed hand trowel to dig the planting holes for this garden, to avoid damaging tree roots. Begin by installing the plants closest to the tree, the 'Sum and Substance' hosta, the 'Elegans' hosta, and the male fern. Spread mulch around them by hand. Be sure to allow sufficient space around the hostas for them to spread to their full size (see "Getting to Know the Plants," beginning on page 62, for details). Give the ferns plenty of room, too, since they will spread.

Step 3: Next, plant the 'Francée' hosta. If you are planting in spring, plant the 'White Christmas' caladiums as you would plant a bulb, about 2 to 3 inches below the surface of the soil, 8 to 12 inches apart. If you are installing your garden in autumn, leave space for the caladiums, but don't plant them until the spring. Mulch around the plants as you go.

Step 4: Install the 'White Nancy' dead nettle and Japanese spurge last. The spacing will depend on whether you use larger plants in containers or small plants in flats; it will also depend on your budget. Planting groundcovers close together, about 4 to 6 inches apart, will give the tree ring a "filled in" appearance in a relatively short time. But plants installed 12 inches apart will eventually fill in, too, it will just take a season or two longer. Mulch the groundcover plants until they fill in and cover the soil—this will take a few years.

Step 5: Water the new transplants carefully over a period of several weeks, making sure each receives about an inch of water a week. Use a soft spray attachment on the hose to prevent the soil from being washed away and try to water early in the day.

CALENDAR OF CARE

SPRING: *If the garden was planted in the autumn, install the caladiums after the new transplants have started to emerge and after the danger of frost is past. Remove any weeds by hand or with a hand fork, and re-apply mulch around the plants if necessary.*

SUMMER: *Keep plants well-watered in the heat of summer, watering early in the day. Rabbits and deer love hostas, so replace any plants that appear to have been eaten (you may want to see if the roots have survived, in which case the plants will be back next year).*

AUTUMN: *After the first frost, cut back all dead foliage and flowers, disposing of undiseased plant waste in a compost heap. Destroy diseased plant remains so they don't contaminate other plants. It can be tricky for beginning gardeners, but you may want to try digging up the caladium tubers, dusting them with a fungicide and storing them in a cool, dry place for the winter. If they appear healthy in spring, try planting them again. The plants won't survive the winter in the ground, so you haven't lost anything if the tubers don't make it. See the alternate plants on page 62 if you'd rather not attempt the tender caladiums at all.*

WINTER: *After the ground has frozen, apply additional mulch (just an inch or two—you don't want to change the grade around the tree roots) to keep plant roots from heaving out of the soil as the weather goes through freeze and thaw cycles.*

GETTING TO KNOW THE PLANTS

'SUM AND SUBSTANCE' HOSTA

I. 'SUM AND SUBSTANCE' HOSTA (*Hosta* x 'Sum and Substance')

CLASSIFICATION: Hardy perennial
PLANT HARDINESS ZONES: 3 to 8
ULTIMATE SIZE: 30" tall and 60" wide (mature plants)
BLOOM TIME: Early to midsummer
SUN REQUIREMENT: Part sun to shade

The individual leaves of this hosta can grow up to 20 inches long and 15 inches wide; each leaf is thick and sturdy. The chartreuse color is a knockout, although the color varies depending on the amount of light the plant receives. 'Sum and Substance' has won many awards from the American Hosta Society since it was first introduced about twenty years ago. It grows quickly, so purchase smaller plants, about 1-gallon size, rather than paying a premium for larger plants.

2. 'ELEGANS' HOSTA

(*Hosta* x 'Elegans', syn. *Hosta sieboldiana* 'Elegans')

CLASSIFICATION: Hardy perennial
PLANT HARDINESS ZONES: 3 to 8
ULTIMATE SIZE: 30" tall and 40" wide, sometimes larger
BLOOM TIME: Early to midsummer
SUN REQUIREMENT: Part sun to shade

'Elegans' is one of the better known "blue" hostas—plants that tend to have thick, well-defined leaves with a distinct blue cast. The leaves of 'Elegans' hosta can reach up to 16 inches long and 12 inches wide.

OTHER RECOMMENDED CULTIVARS
Other medium to giant-sized blue hostas include:
• 'Blue Mammoth' • 'Bressingham Blue' • 'Big Daddy'
• 'Krossa Regal' • 'Hadspen Blue'

'ELEGANS' HOSTA

MALE FERN

3. MALE FERN (*Dryopteris filix-mas*)

CLASSIFICATION: Hardy perennial
PLANT HARDINESS ZONES: 3 to 8
ULTIMATE SIZE: To 4' tall and 3' wide
BLOOM TIME: Foliage plant; flowers insignificant
SUN REQUIREMENT: Part to full shade

Ferns are one of the easiest plants to grow in a shady garden, especially if the soil is moist and rich in organic matter. The large, arching leaves of the male fern are lush and attractive background plants, growing vigorously without spreading excessively. There are many ferns with similar characteristics, but the male fern is very hardy and reliable.

'WHITE CHRISTMAS' CALADIUM

4. 'WHITE CHRISTMAS' CALADIUM
(*Caladium* x 'White Christmas')

CLASSIFICATION: Tropical annual (sometimes listed as a bulb)
PLANT HARDINESS ZONES: 8 to 10
ULTIMATE SIZE: To about 2'–3' tall and wide
BLOOM TIME: Foliage plant; flowers insignificant
SUN REQUIREMENT: Part sun to part shade

This South American native has long been grown as a houseplant, but in recent years it has been recognized as a valuable foliage plant for the garden. Caladiums that are sold in pots as houseplants may not make the transition to the garden successfully. Look for potted caladiums sold as outdoor plants, or purchase the tuberous rhizomes wherever you would shop for flowering bulbs. Since they flower from late spring through summer, spring is the best time to plant caladium tubers.

CALADIUM SUBSTITUTES

For those who don't want to bother with caladiums, an easy alternative is to plant annual white flowering tobacco (*Nicotiana alata*) in seed form, in flats, or in 3- to 4-inch pots. A perennial alternative is to substitute hostas with predominantly white leaves, such as 'Paul's Glory' hosta, 'Loyalist' hosta, or 'Gay Feather' hosta.

5. 'FRANCEE' HOSTA (*Hosta* x 'Francée')

CLASSIFICATION: Hardy perennial
PLANT HARDINESS ZONES: 3 to 8
ULTIMATE SIZE: To 24" tall and 36" wide
BLOOM TIME: Early to midsummer
SUN REQUIREMENT: Part sun to shade

'Francee' has been consistently popular ever since it was first introduced. The neat mounds of crisp green foliage edged with white margins are especially nice when mass planted. 'Francee' has spawned a tissue-cultured sport called 'Patriot', which has much wider white margins on green leaves, making this plant a stand-out in shadier gardens. Although established hostas can be divided to give you new plants, they achieve a better appearance if they are allowed to mature without division for up to five years.

'FRANCÉE' HOSTA

6. 'WHITE NANCY' DEAD NETTLE, SPOTTED DEAD NETTLE   (*Lamium maculatum* 'White Nancy')

CLASSIFICATION: Perennial groundcover
PLANT HARDINESS ZONES: 3 to 8
ULTIMATE SIZE: To about 8" tall, spreading
BLOOM TIME: Late spring through summer
SUN REQUIREMENT: Part sun to shade

Like many plants in the mint family, lamium can become invasive (not always a bad thing in a groundcover). Cultivars such as 'White Nancy' appear to be more restrained than the species. The variegated leaves are silvery white and green, with pure white flowers that are especially valuable in shady areas. (Lamium is also one of the few plants that will tolerate dry shade.) Lamium does not always perform well in hot climates or in full sun, so plant it where there is cool shade or some form of shelter.

'WHITE NANCY' DEAD NETTLE

CULTIVAR SUBSTITUTES
• 'Beacon Silver'—pink-flowering; better in hot climates, but less hardy in cool ones
• 'Chequers'—variegated, violet-flowered • 'Aureum'—gold leaves and pink flowers • 'Shell Pink'—large pink flowers and white-splashed leaves
• 'Pink Pewter'—pink flowers and white-washed green leaves • 'Beedham's White'—white flowers, yellow foliage • 'Album'—variegated leaves, white flowers

JAPANESE SPURGE

7. JAPANESE SPURGE   (*Pachysandra terminalis*)

CLASSIFICATION: Perennial groundcover
PLANT HARDINESS ZONES: 5 to 9
ULTIMATE SIZE: To about 8" tall, spreading
BLOOM TIME: Foliage plant; flowers insignificant
SUN REQUIREMENT: Sun to shade

Japanese spurge or pachysandra is an excellent groundcover as well as one of the few that can survive in heavy shade. The attractive foliage is a crisp, glossy green; it quickly forms a dense mat. Some weeding may be necessary until pachysandra becomes established, but once it fills in it needs little maintenance and will crowd out most weeds. Pachysandra will grow in full sun but the leaves may turn yellow and burn; it is preferable to plant it where there is at least partial protection from the hot sun, especially when plants are young. To encourage pachysandra to fill in quickly, plant rooted cuttings 6 to 8 inches apart and keep the soil evenly moist.

A GARDEN FOR A CORNER OF THE YARD

This garden was designed to have the biggest impact in spring to early summer, with the garden sited in a mainly sunny spot that may get a little shade. The majority of the plants are best planted in the autumn, with the possible exception of 'The Fairy' polyantha rose. This is a very hardy rose, but if there is any doubt about its winter hardiness in your area, wait until spring to plant it.

This corner garden can also be planted as an island bed, built up on a berm about 8 to 12 inches above the grade of the soil. Planting the tree above the soil line can improve drainage; by raising the bed above the level of the soil and digging with a sharp, spaded edge you also keep grass out of the planting area. Apply mulch to this planting area to help control weeds and to protect plant roots over the winter.

I selected 'Prairie Fire' flowering crabapple for the centerpiece of this garden because of its hardiness, disease resistance, attractive foliage, beautiful flowers, and colorful fruits. If you already have a compact, ornamental, spring-flowering tree in your yard, go ahead and work the design around your existing tree.

YOU WILL NEED...

- A square-ended spade if sod has to be removed

- A garden fork to loosen the soil

- A round-pointed shovel for planting the tree, rose, shrubs, and any gallon-size or larger containers of perennials

- A narrow-bladed hand trowel for planting the forget-me-nots, sweet woodruff, and cranesbill geraniums

- A wheelbarrow for moving soil, sod, plants, and debris

- Amendments to soil if needed or desired: peat moss, shredded leaves, sand, aged manure, or compost, for example

- Mulch, as needed, to spread to a depth of 3 inches around the plants when installed

- Pruning shears to cut away any dead, diseased, or damaged branches or flowers

- Lopping shears to prune shoots that sprout from the base of crabapple trees, as well as broken or crossed branches

- Garden gloves and garden shoes or boots

- A kneeling pad

PLANT LIST

1. 'Prairie Fire' flowering crabapple (*Malus* x 'Prairie Fire')

2. Forget-me-not (*Myosotis scorpiodes*)

3. Sweet woodruff (*Galium odoratum*)

4. 'Mohawk' viburnum (*Viburnum burkwoodii* 'Mohawk')

5. 'Pink Princess' peony (*Paeonia* x 'Pink Princess')

6. Dwarf fothergilla (*Fothergilla gardenii*)

7. 'The Fairy' polyantha rose (*Rosa* x 'The Fairy')

8. 'Johnson's Blue' cranesbill geranium (*Geranium himalayense* 'Johnson's Blue')

A GARDEN FOR A CORNER OF THE YARD

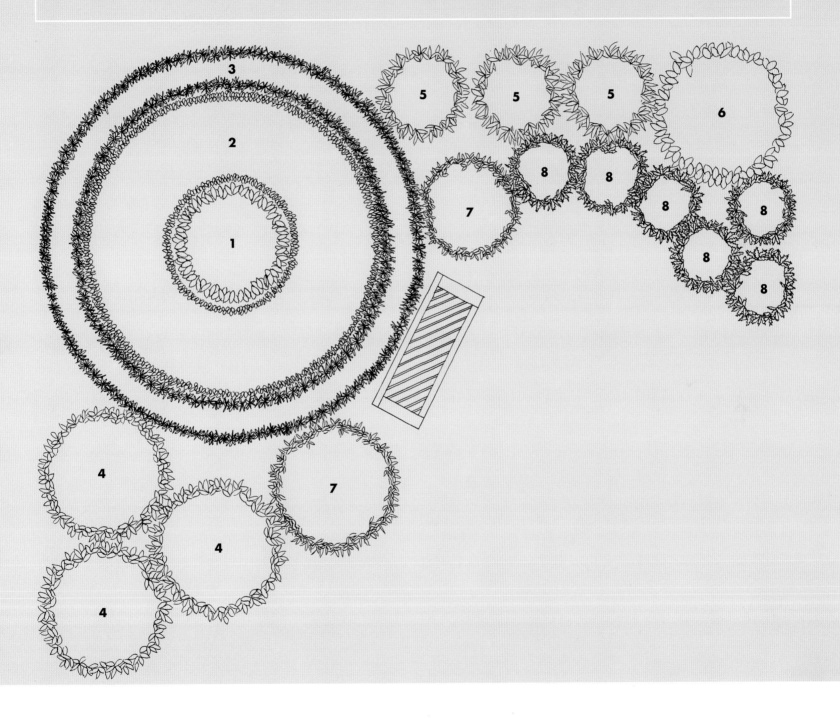

PLANTING THE GARDEN FOR A CORNER OF THE YARD, STEP BY STEP

Step 1: Follow the steps on page 10–11 that deal with preparing the planting area and digging the planting holes. Plant this garden in the autumn, in full sun to part shade, so the roots will have time to become established before flowering. If you live in Zone 5 or farther north, plant 'The Fairy' rose in spring so it can become established before the cold winter months. Do not fertilize at planting time.

Step 2: Install the 'Prairie Fire' crabapple first. If you've purchased bareroot by mail order, just remove any packing materials from the roots and soak them in a bucket of water 24 hours before planting. If you are purchasing from a nursery, note that a balled and burlapped crabapple rather than one grown in a container will give the best results.

Place the tree or shrub into the planting hole on top of the loosened soil. Begin filling in around the sides of the plant with the soil set aside when the hole was dug. Never install plants deeper in the hole than they were planted at the nursery (you can usually see a mark on the trunk to show where the soil level was). Plant the tree or shrub high enough to allow for settling in the planting hole. Once all the soil has been filled in, create a hollow in the soil around the trunk or base of the plant. This will direct water right to the root zone.

Step 3: Plant the viburnums, the fothergilla, and roses in the same way you planted the crabapple, mulching and pruning dead branches as you go.

Step 4: Next, plant the peonies with the "eye" of each plant just an inch or so beneath the soil. Spread the roots out in the planting hole, carefully replacing the soil on top of the roots.

Step 5: Finally, install the cranesbill geraniums, forget-me-nots, and sweet woodruff, spreading the mulch around each plant carefully by hand.

Step 6: Water the garden well after all the plants have been installed. Keep the plants well watered until they become established. Each plant should receive about an inch of water a week in its root zone. Use a soft spray attachment on the hose to prevent the soil from being washed away. Water early in the day, before the sun is at its peak.

CALENDAR OF CARE

SPRING: *The peony will probably not need support in its first year, but by the second year you might want to install peony hoops in the spring after the red shoots have unfurled and the green foliage begins to grow. Do not be alarmed if you see ants on the peonies; the ants apparently help the peonies to open. Apply a granular rose fertilizer around the base of the rose bushes, working it into the soil with a garden fork or hand fork. In early spring, prune back the roses to within a foot or two from the ground.*

SUMMER: *Cut back the peony foliage when it becomes unsightly—sometimes in summer, sometimes not until the autumn. Apply additional rose fertilizer in June and July, but none later than that. Prune the roses and remove dead blossoms to encourage repeat bloom.*

AUTUMN: *After the first frost, cut back all dead foliage of perennials; dispose of undiseased plant waste in a compost heap. Destroy diseased plant remains so they don't contaminate other plants. Prune back the shrubs to improve their shape, if desired. Clean blades carefully, especially after trimming diseased leaves or branches. Prune unsightly shoots from the base of the crabapple in late autumn; also remove any crossed or broken branches.*

WINTER: *After the ground has frozen, apply additional mulch (no more than 3 inches deep) to keep plant roots from heaving out of the soil as the weather goes through freeze and thaw cycles.*

GETTING TO KNOW THE PLANTS

'PRAIRIE FIRE' FLOWERING CRABAPPLE

1. 'PRAIRIE FIRE' FLOWERING CRABAPPLE   (*Malus* x 'Prairie Fire', syn. 'Prairifire')

CLASSIFICATION: Ornamental tree
PLANT HARDINESS ZONES: 4 to 8
ULTIMATE SIZE: Approximately 20' tall and wide
BLOOM TIME: Late spring or early summer
SUN REQUIREMENT: Full sun

In an evaluation of crabapples by Ohio State University's Ohio Agricultural Research and Development Center, 'Prairie Fire' crabapple was described as having "spectacular bloom with flowers contrasting with emerging red-tinged green foliage." The tree is upright when young but becomes more rounded and spreading with age, so give it room to grow. The foliage emerges as a dark purple-red, gradually turning dark green over the summer. The dark purple-red fruit is attractive and persists through the winter.

2. FORGET-ME-NOT

(*Myosotis scorpiodes*, syn. *M. palustris*)

CLASSIFICATION: Hardy perennial
PLANT HARDINESS ZONES: 3 to 8
ULTIMATE SIZE: To 8" tall and wide
BLOOM TIME: Late spring until frost
SUN REQUIREMENT: Part sun to part shade

One of several flowers called "forget-me-not," this plant is probably the most ornamental; it is referred to as the "true" forget-me-not. It is a spreading, water-loving woodland plant that performs well in part sun to part shade as long as sufficient water is provided. The tiny flowers are a lovely blue with a tinier yellow eye; they bloom profusely in spring and then less profusely until frost.

FORGET-ME-NOT

SWEET WOODRUFF

3. SWEET WOODRUFF

(*Galium odoratum*, syn. *Asperula odorata*)

CLASSIFICATION: Hardy perennial groundcover
PLANT HARDINESS ZONES: 4 to 8
ULTIMATE SIZE: To about 8" tall and 15" wide, spreading
BLOOM TIME: Late spring to early summer
SUN REQUIREMENT: Part sun to part shade

Although sweet woodruff is classified as a groundcover, it is a delicate-looking plant that may take a year or two to fill in, and even then it may not be dense enough to completely crowd out weeds. Still, it is a wonderful addition to any garden that offers a little shade and consistently moist soil. The small leaves are neat and very ornamental throughout the season; when the tiny sprays of white flowers bloom they seem to hover just above the foliage. The fact that it is shallow-rooted makes sweet woodruff a good choice to plant under shrubs that don't like much root competition. Both the foliage and flowers boast a delicate fragrance.

'MOHAWK' VIBURNUM

4. 'MOHAWK' VIBURNUM
Viburnum burkwoodii 'Mohawk')

CLASSIFICATION: Ornamental shrub
PLANT HARDINESS ZONES: 5 to 8
ULTIMATE SIZE: To 10' tall and 6' wide
BLOOM TIME: Spring
SUN REQUIREMENT: Sun to part shade

'Mohawk' viburnum is beautiful in bud and in bloom, and is especially valued for its wonderful clove-like fragrance. Because 'Mohawk' is equally attractive in bud as when it is in full bloom, the season of interest is much longer than that of most flowering shrubs. It also has clean, disease-resistant foliage that turns a vivid red-orange in the autumn. 'Mohawk' is usually more compact that indicated above, but some specimens do become quite large so it is best to plant this shrub where it will have room to grow.

5. 'PINK PRINCESS' PEONY
(*Paeonia* x 'Pink Princess', syn. 'Pink Dawn')

CLASSIFICATION: Hardy perennial
PLANT HARDINESS ZONES: 3 to 7
ULTIMATE SIZE: To 3' tall and wide
BLOOM TIME: Late spring to early summer
SUN REQUIREMENT: Full sun

Peonies are old-fashioned flowers that have regained popularity. They are extremely long-lived but don't like being moved. The huge flowers are often so heavy that they need firm support—a specially made peony hoop is one of the most efficient methods. Plant peonies in full sun in moist but well-drained soil. 'Pink Princess' is just one of countless excellent peonies; its clear pink flowers are brushed with a darker, rosy pink and the brilliant gold stamens at the center add to its attraction.

'PINK PRINCESS' PEONY

6. DWARF FOTHERGILLA *(Fothergilla gardenii)*

CLASSIFICATION: Hardy shrub
PLANT HARDINESS ZONES: 5 to 8
ULTIMATE SIZE: 3' tall and wide, sometimes larger
BLOOM TIME: Spring
SUN REQUIREMENT: Sun to part shade

Fothergilla is one of the stars of the spring garden, with interesting white bottlebrush flowers with the fragrance of honey. The green foliage has a slight blue cast, most prominently in the cultivar 'Blue Mist'. In autumn, fothergilla once again moves to center stage as its leaves light up in a flame-colored blaze of yellow, red, and orange. Fothergilla flowers best in full sun although it will also do well in part shade. Plant it in moist, well-drained soil that has an acid pH.

DWARF FOTHERGILLA

CUSTOMIZING TIP

IF YOU HAVE MATURE TREES

If your garden has mature existing trees that do not let in much sunlight, substitute an understory tree for the crabapple. Consider a pink/purple flowering redbud, a large-flowering rhododendron, or a yellow-flowering 'Golden Glory' corneliancherry dogwood (*Cornus mas*). Replace the polyantha rose with a small-leaved azalea and the peony with a hybrid bleeding heart (*Dicentra* x 'Luxuriant'). The existing shrubs will work in part shade.

'THE FAIRY' POLYANTHA ROSE

7. 'THE FAIRY' POLYANTHA ROSE
(*Rosa* x 'The Fairy')

CLASSIFICATION: Hardy polyantha rose
PLANT HARDINESS ZONES: 5 to 9
ULTIMATE SIZE: To 3 feet tall and wide
BLOOM TIME: Late spring, early summer, with repeat
  bloom through autumn
SUN REQUIREMENT: Full sun

Polyantha means "many flowered," which is a good description of this hardy rose. 'The Fairy' blooms later than some roses, but it is worth the wait because of its consistent reblooming habit. The pink flowers are small but prolific, covering the small shrub with buds and blooms. This is one of the easiest roses to care for, although, like all roses, it likes lots of sun, water, and regular fertilization. Even though 'The Fairy' is quite hardy—mulching the roots may be all the protection it needs—it is also a proven performer in hot climates.

8. 'JOHNSON'S BLUE' CRANESBILL GERANIUM

(*Geranium* x 'Johnson's Blue', syn. *G. himalayense*
'Johnson's Blue')

CLASSIFICATION: Hardy perennial
PLANT HARDINESS ZONES: 4 to 9
ULTIMATE SIZE: To 2' tall and wide
BLOOM TIME: Late spring to early summer
SUN REQUIREMENT: Full sun to part shade

These are not the geraniums so often seen with brilliant red flowers primly displayed in terra-cotta pots. Cranesbill geraniums are sprawling, low-growing plants that look great spilling onto a path or edging a mixed border. Most cranesbills flower best in full sun but will perform equally well in part shade in moist, well-drained soil; some can even survive deep shade. While the flower color in cranesbills ranges from white to pale pink to rosy pink to purples, and even hot fuchsias and magentas, 'Johnson's Blue' is the only cranesbill in cultivation that has the blue flowers so coveted by gardeners.

'JOHNSON'S BLUE' CRANESBILL

CUSTOMIZING TIP

FOR THE SOUTHWEST

For a tough southwestern garden, replace the dwarf fothergilla with the heat-tolerant western sandcherry (*Prunus besseyi*) and use a Texas mountain laurel (*Sophora secundiflora*) in place of the crabapple. Many roses love the desert heat of the southwest, so replace the 'Mohawk' viburnums with a medium-sized fragrant rose such as the pink-to-red-flowered 'Archduke Charles' or the pale pink, repeat-blooming 'Souvenir de Malmaison'. 'The Fairy' rose will work in the Southwest, but substitute snow-in-summer (*Cerastium tomentosum*) for the forget-me-nots. Instead of sweet woodruff, use creeping thyme (*Thymus serpyllum*), and instead of cranesbill geraniums, plant rock rose (*Helianthemum nummularium*). Some peonies will perform well in the Southwest; if in doubt go for a native Texan such as guara (*Gaura lindheimeri*), planting a group of three in place of the peony. This long-blooming perennial has white with pink flowers; the new 'Siskiyou Pink' cultivar has light pink with darker rosy pink flowers.

A PASTEL MAILBOX GARDEN

This garden was designed with a streetside rural or suburban mailbox in mind, but you might change the shape of the plan and use the design around a lamp post or even as an island bed with a garden ornament in the middle. While the accompanying plan uses a rectangular-shaped layout, it can easily be modified into a curved or crescent-shaped planting area. Keep the lower-growing plants along the edges and in the front of the mailbox, with vines and taller flowers growing around the mailbox post and at the back of the bed. The plant height should be layered in steps from low to medium to tall.

The flowering vines will climb the mailbox post and eventually creep over the box itself, but the vines will initially need more support than just the post, so this plan calls for a small trellis to be braced against the back of the post. As an alternative to the trellis, a piece of chicken wire about 2 feet tall can be wrapped around the base of the post.

YOU WILL NEED...

- A square-ended spade if sod has to be removed

- A garden fork to loosen the soil

- A round-pointed shovel for planting the rose and any gallon-size or larger containers of perennials

- A broad-bladed hand trowel for planting smaller perennials, if needed

- A hand fork for planting the morning glory seeds

- A wheelbarrow for moving soil, sod, plants, and debris

- Amendments to soil if needed or desired: peat moss, shredded leaves, sand, aged manure, or compost, for example

- Mulch, as needed, to spread to a depth of 3 inches around the plants when installed

- Pruning shears to cut away any dead, diseased, or damaged branches or flowers and to prune the rose

- Garden gloves and garden shoes or boots

- Rubber or leather garden gloves to protect from rose thorns

- A trellis or chicken wire to support the vines

- Stakes and string or a peony hoop (not needed until second year)

- Granular rose fertilizer

PLANT LIST

1. 'Ramona' clematis (*Clematis* x 'Ramona')

2. 'Heavenly Blue' morning glory (*Ipomoea tricolor* 'Heavenly Blue')

3. 'Clara Curtis' chrysanthemum (*Chrysanthemum rubellum* 'Clara Curtis')

4. 'Sunny Border Blue' speedwell (*Veronica* x 'Sunny Border Blue')

5. 'Pink Lemonade' peony (*Paeonia* x 'Pink Lemonade')

6. 'Silver Mound' artemisia (*Artemisia schmidtiana* 'Silver Mound')

7. 'Ballerina' hybrid musk rose (*Rosa* x 'Ballerina')

8. 'Hidcote' lavender (*Lavandula angustifolia* 'Hidcote')

A PASTEL MAILBOX GARDEN

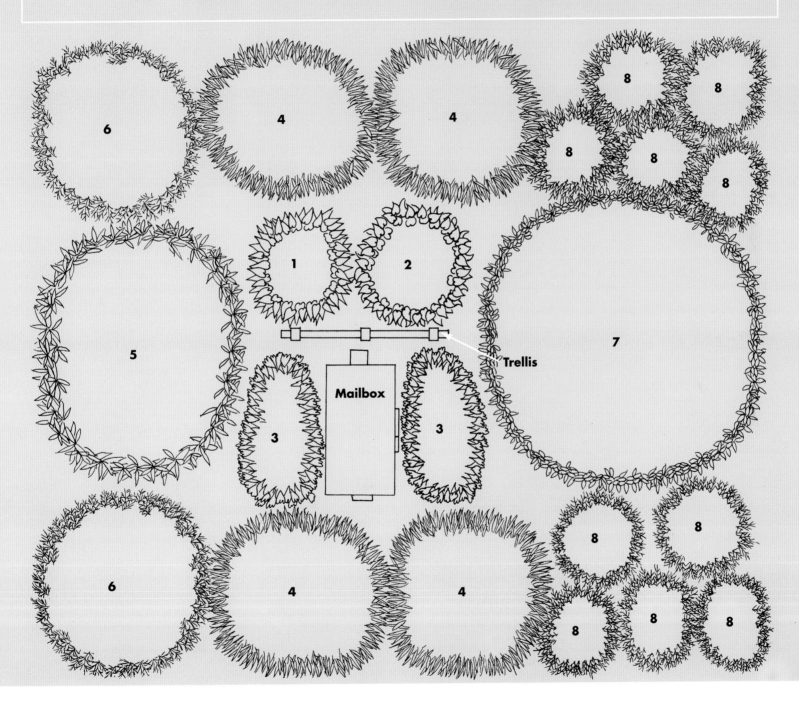

PLANTING THE PASTEL MAILBOX GARDEN, STEP BY STEP

Step 1: Follow the steps on page 10–11 that deal with preparing the planting area and digging the planting holes. Install this garden in the spring after danger of frost is past; the plants will perform best in full sun.

Step 2: Plant the clematis first, placing it about 6 inches in front of the trellis (or other form of support). If the tendrils are long enough, push them carefully through the support or trellis; this will encourage the clematis to weave through the trellis as it climbs. You will need to periodically push new growth through the supports in the same manner.

Step 3: Next, plant the morning glory seeds directly into the soil around the trellis, on the opposite side of the clematis. Use a hand fork to create furrows in the soil; drop the large morning glory seeds into the furrows. Instead of thinning the seeds later, plant only about six to ten seeds here, and save the rest to plant elsewhere in the garden. Use the back of a level-headed rake to pull and smooth the soil over the seedlings. Apply a handful or two of mulch on top of the newly planted seeds—no more than

that. Keep the seeds well-watered until the young plant is tall enough to twine through the trellis or support.

Step 4: Next plant the rose, wearing heavy gloves to protect yourself from thorns. Prune away any broken or diseased-looking branches. After planting and mulching the roses, work some granular rose fertilizer into the soil a few inches from the base of the plant, using a hand fork.

Step 5: Plant the peony, setting the "eye" on a mound of soil with the roots spread out around it, then carefully filling in the soil so that the eye remains only about an inch below the soil surface. After the first year, a peony hoop or other form of staking will probably be necessary to support the heavy blossoms. Install the hoop or stakes while the foliage is still emerging in spring, and remove the hoop when the foliage is cut back in late summer or autumn.

Step 6: Finally, install the remaining perennials, the chrysanthemum, speedwell, artemisia, and lavender, removing any weeds and stones from the bed and pruning any dead or damaged foliage as you go. Use a scoop or pitchfork to bring mulch to the bed, but work it around each plant by hand. Be sure to leave a hollow around the base of each plant so water will be directed to the root zone. Water well until the plants have become established.

CALENDAR OF CARE

SPRING: *Remove winter mulch from the base of plants; install new mulch as needed to help discourage weed germination. Pull weeds as soon as they appear, before the roots have time to spread. Apply granular rose fertilizer around the base of the rose bush. Prune back the rose to a foot or two above the ground. Plant morning glory seeds once the danger of frost is past. Prune any broken branches from the clematis and refasten to trellis as needed. Fertilize perennials, if desired, using a slow-release "bloom buster" formula.*

SUMMER: *Provide extra support for the vines, if necessary, using foam-covered wire to fasten heavy branches to the trellis. Continue training new tendrils through the supports. Pinch back the foliage of the chrysanthemums to keep them neat and compact. Remove the peony foliage when it becomes unsightly, in late summer or autumn, and remove the peony hoop or stakes. Reapply rose fertilizer; reapply perennial fertilizer if desired, but no later than midsummer. Prune the rose and remove dead blossoms to encourage repeat bloom; trim or shear the artemisia and lavender to keep the shape neat, if needed.*

AUTUMN: *After the first frost, cut back all dead foliage; dispose of undiseased plant waste in a compost heap. The morning glory is an annual, and will not come up the following year, so you can pull it up from the roots—just be careful not to damage the clematis vine or roots when doing so. Destroy diseased plant remains so they don't contaminate other plants. Prune back the shrubs to improve their shape, if desired. Clean blades carefully, especially after trimming diseased leaves or branches.*

WINTER: *After the ground has frozen, apply additional mulch (no more than 3 inches deep) to keep plant roots from heaving out of the soil as the weather goes through freeze and thaw cycles.*

GETTING TO KNOW THE PLANTS

'RAMONA' CLEMATIS

1. 'RAMONA' CLEMATIS   (*Clematis* x 'Ramona')

CLASSIFICATION: Perennial vine
PLANT HARDINESS ZONES: 4 to 8
ULTIMATE SIZE: To 15' tall
BLOOM TIME: Summer, followed by ornamental seedheads
SUN REQUIREMENT: Full sun with protected or shaded roots

The huge flowers of clematis are breathtaking, but both the flowers and the twining, vining foliage are delicate enough that they can be trained up through other shrubs and trees, as well as against moderately sturdy arbors, fences, and trellises. 'Ramona' clematis has large, lavender-blue flowers that blend well with many other garden plants. Clematis does best in full sun, but create some shade to protect the roots—either install foliage plants around the base of the vine, or create shade with garden ornaments.

OTHER LARGE-FLOWERED CLEMATIS
The countless large-flowered clematis forms include:
'Henryii'—pure white • 'Nelly Moser'—light pink petals with dark rose stripes • 'Vyvyan Pennell'—pale lilac, double-flowered • 'Niobe'—ruby-purple • 'Moonlight'—creamy, almost yellow • 'Ville de Lyon'—deep pink-red

2. 'HEAVENLY BLUE' MORNING GLORY
(*Ipomea tricolor* 'Heavenly Blue')

CLASSIFICATION: Annual vine
PLANT HARDINESS ZONES: 8 to 10
ULTIMATE SIZE: To 10' tall
BLOOM TIME: All summer
SUN REQUIREMENT: Full sun to part shade

Morning glories are fast-growing annuals that can be started from seed indoors or sown directly into the planting bed once the chance of frost is past. The flowers open early in the day and close in the hot afternoon sun (but remain open when it is overcast). Be careful not to overfertilize morning glories or you will have a huge, leaf-covered vine and very few flowers. Average soil, occasional watering, and a sunny site are all these annuals demand. Morning glories occasionally self-seed but usually need to be replanted each year.

'HEAVENLY BLUE' MORNING GLORY

'CLARA CURTIS' CHRYSANTHEMUM

3. 'CLARA CURTIS' CHRYSANTHEMUM
(*Chrysanthemum rubellum* 'Clara Curtis', syn. *Chrysanthemum zawadskii* var. *latilobum* 'Clara Curtis', syn. *Dendranthema zawadskii* 'Clara Curtis')

CLASSIFICATION: Hardy perennial
PLANT HARDINESS ZONES: 4 to 10
ULTIMATE SIZE: To 3' tall and 2' wide
BLOOM TIME: Midsummer with repeat bloom
    through autumn
SUN REQUIREMENT: Full to part sun

The flowers of 'Clara Curtis' chrysanthemum look more like small pink yellow-centered daisies than traditional chrysanthemum flowers, but they are just as hardy, reliable, and easy to grow. 'Clara Curtis' may occasionally get tall enough to require staking, but if you pinch back the foliage in late spring it will keep the plant dense and compact. Plant chrysanthemums in a sunny spot with average soil, deadhead occasionally to encourage repeat bloom, and water well until the new plants are established.

'Sunny Border Blue' speedwell

4. 'SUNNY BORDER BLUE' SPEEDWELL

(*Veronica* x 'Sunny Border Blue', syn. *V. longifolia* 'Sunny Border Blue')

CLASSIFICATION: Hardy perennial
PLANT HARDINESS ZONES: 3 to 8
ULTIMATE SIZE: To 2' tall and wide
BLOOM TIME: Late spring to early summer with repeat bloom
SUN REQUIREMENT: Full sun

The spiky flowers of speedwell add an interesting vertical accent to the mixed perennial garden. There are many species, hybrids, and cultivars with slightly different forms and with colors ranging from white to rose to pink to purple to all shades of blue. 'Sunny Border Blue' is a beautiful and reliable hybrid that performs well in a sunny spot with well-drained soil.

OTHER GOOD CULTIVARS
Other excellent speedwells include:
- *Veronica latifolia* 'Crater Lake Blue' • *V. spicata* 'Icicle'—white-flowered
- *V. spicata* 'Blue Peter'—very compact • *V. spicata* 'Red Fox'—rosy red flowers

5. 'PINK LEMONADE' PEONY   (*Paeonia* x 'Pink Lemonade')

CLASSIFICATION: Hardy perennial
PLANT HARDINESS ZONES: 3 to 7
ULTIMATE SIZE: To 3' tall and wide
BLOOM TIME: Midsummer
SUN REQUIREMENT: Full sun

Peonies have been a garden favorite for years, in part because they are easy to grow and incredibly long-lived. Probably the biggest reason that peonies continue to thrill garden lovers is that their huge, abundant flowers are beyond compare. 'Pink Lemonade' has large, pale pink, yellow, and cream "bomb"-type flowers that bloom later in the season than other peonies; it is mildly fragrant.

'Pink Lemonade' peony

'SILVER MOUND' ARTEMISIA

6. 'SILVER MOUND' ARTEMISIA, WORMWOOD   (*Artemisia schmidtiana* 'Silver Mound')

CLASSIFICATION: Hardy perennial herb
PLANT HARDINESS ZONES: 4 to 10
ULTIMATE SIZE: To 2' tall and wide
BLOOM TIME: Flowers not ornamental
SUN REQUIREMENT: Full sun

This is one of the most restrained forms of the wormwood family, growing in compact mounds of silvery gray foliage that looks as soft as silk and almost begs to be touched—'Silver Mound' is easy to find and easy to grow. Although 'Silver Mound' tends to stay compact, it may need occasional trimming to keep the rounded shape from sprawling. Plant in full sun in average soil; once established, it is very drought tolerant, but water well when first planted.

'BALLERINA' HYBRID MUSK ROSE

7. 'BALLERINA' HYBRID MUSK ROSE (*Rosa* x 'Ballerina')

CLASSIFICATION: Hardy rose
PLANT HARDINESS ZONES: 4 to 9
ULTIMATE SIZE: To 4' tall and wide
BLOOM TIME: Early summer with repeat bloom
SUN REQUIREMENT: Full sun

Although the flowers of 'Ballerina' are small—only about 2 inches across—they cover this shrub so profusely in early summer that it looks like a pink waterfall. It has an arching form that is distinctive and very attractive if pruned occasionally to keep it from getting shaggy. There is repeat flowering on and off throughout the summer, but never reaching the intensity of the first bloom. The flowers have yellow stamens surrounded by a white center. The outer edges of the petals are a pale pink, and the buds are a medium pink. 'Ballerina' is disease resistant and quite cold hardy; it is also slightly fragrant.

8. 'HIDCOTE' LAVENDER (*Lavandula angustifolia* 'Hidcote')

CLASSIFICATION: Shrubby perennial herb
PLANT HARDINESS ZONES: 5 to 8
ULTIMATE SIZE: To 2' tall and wide
BLOOM TIME: Midsummer through autumn
SUN REQUIREMENT: Full sun

Lavender is one of the best-known herbs; its aromatic foliage and flowers dry well and are found in potpourris, perfumes, sachets, teas, and sleep pillows as well as a wide range of medicinal and cosmetic products. In the garden, they are compact, shrubby plants that can be grown as specimens, massed at the edge of a flower border, or sheared into a low hedge. The dark-purple flowering 'Hidcote' is a familiar plant in English gardens, but it is also hardy enough for most regions of North America.

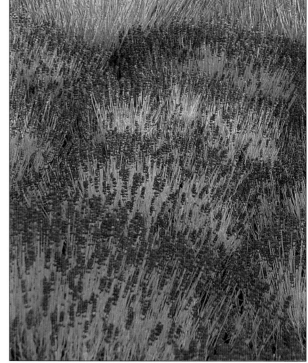

'HIDCOTE' LAVENDER

A MAILBOX GARDEN OF ANNUALS

The garden plan can be easily modified to create an annual garden, if you do not feel ready to commit to perennials yet. The problem with annuals is that they last only one season, so need to be replanted every year. Some gardeners like this idea—it means they can experiment with new colors and displays every year. Some annuals do self-seed, appearing in the garden year after year, but it is usually easy to mulch over or pull out the young seedlings if they aren't wanted.

To make a mailbox garden design using annuals, substitute the following plants for the plants of the same number in the plan:

1. Hyacinth bean vine (*Dolichos lablab* syn. *Lablab purpureus*)—Start from seed, sowing the seeds directly into the soil after the chance of frost is past.

2. Morning glory (*Ipomea tricolor* 'Heavenly Blue')—same as featured in main plan

3. Starcluster (*Pentas* spp.), lantana (*Lantana camara*), or china aster (*Callistephus chinensis*) *Note:* These plants may be considered perennial in the South.

4. 'Victoria' salvia (*Salvia farinacea* 'Victoria')

5. 'Loveliness' mallow (*Lavatera trimestris* 'Loveliness') or large-flowered zinnia (*Zinnia* spp.)

6. Dusty miller (*Senecio cineraria*)—This plant will often survive a mild winter, so you may want to cut it back rather than pulling out the whole plant in the autumn.

7. Spiderflowers (*Cleome hasslerana*) or old-fashioned cosmos (*Cosmos bipinnata* 'Sensation')—You will need a large stand of either of these in order to replace the mass of the rosebush.

8. 'Lavender Lady' globe amaranth (*Gomphrena globosa* 'Lavender Lady')—a very hardy and drought-resistant plant

A FRAGRANT EVENING GARDEN

There is not much point in having a fragrant evening garden if you don't have a place to sit and enjoy it. For this reason, this garden is designed around a bench beneath a vine-covered arbor, but it could also be adapted to encircle a deck or patio.

Both the clematis and wisteria start slow for the first few years, but by the second year the clematis will be flowering nicely and by the third year it will start covering one side of the arbor. The wisteria may take five years to bloom, but it will be phenomenal when it does. Wisteria twines naturally, so rather than tying the vine to train it, simply encourage it to twine around the arbor posts. Wisteria eventually becomes heavy and requires the support of a strong, sturdy trellis. If you don't want to make that kind of an investment, plant the fragrant, fast-growing but more delicate *Clematis montana* 'Rubens' instead. Plant the Chilean jasmine, flowering tobacco, and regal lily in spring; the rest can be installed in spring or autumn.

YOU WILL NEED...

- A square-ended spade if sod has to be removed, also for digging a straight-edged hole for the tree, if desired

- A garden fork to loosen the soil

- A round-pointed shovel for planting the crabapple, rose, shrubs, and any gallon-size or larger containers of perennials

- A broad-bladed hand trowel for planting the lily and smaller perennials, if needed

- A narrow-bladed hand trowel for installing container plants and flats of flowering tobacco (if not available in larger containers)

- A wheelbarrow for moving soil, sod, plants, and debris

- Amendments to soil if needed or desired: peat moss, shredded leaves, sand, aged manure, or compost, for example

- Mulch, as needed, to spread to a depth of 3 inches around the plants when installed

- Pruning shears to cut away any dead, diseased, or damaged branches or flowers

- Garden gloves and garden shoes or boots

- Rubber or leather gloves to protect from rose thorns

- Two large urns or containers for the Chilean jasmine

- Commercial potting mixture suitable for container use

- Arbor and bench

- Dry granular rose fertilizer

- Dry granular fertilizer for container plants, flowering-plant formula

PLANT LIST

1. Chilean jasmine (*Mandevilla laxa*)

2. Henry clematis (*Clematis* x *henryii*)

3. White Chinese wisteria (*Wisteria sinensis* 'Alba')

4. Koreanspice viburnum (*Viburnum carlesii*)

5. 'Blanc Double de Coubert' hybrid rugosa rose (*Rosa* x 'Blanc Double de Coubert')

6. Variegated sweet mock orange (*Philadelphus coronarius* 'Variegatus')

7. Flowering tobacco (*Nicotiana alata*)

8. Regal lily (*Lilium regale*)

9. Tufted evening primrose (*Oenothera caespitosa*)

10. 'Plantaginea' hosta (*Hosta* x 'Plantaginea')

11. 'Satin Cloud' crabapple (*Malus* x 'Satin Cloud')

A FRAGRANT EVENING GARDEN

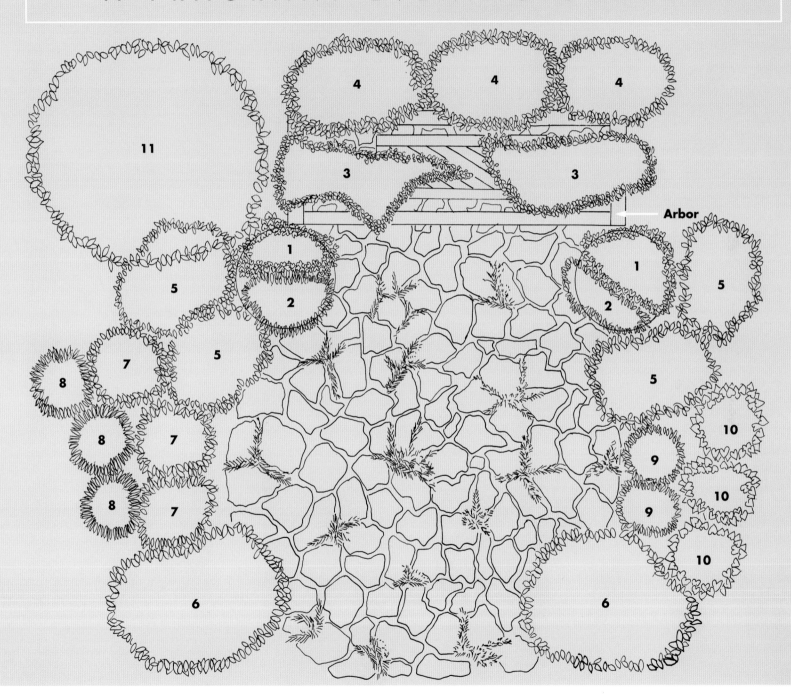

Arbor

PLANTING THE FRAGRANT EVENING GARDEN, STEP BY STEP

Step 1: Install a bench and arbor to suit your needs and budget. If you wish to create a path leading to the bench, you can make an inexpensive one by removing sod and excavating about 6 inches of topsoil. Use about 2 inches of construction sand as a base, and top it with pea gravel or mulch to a depth of 3 to 4 inches.

Step 2: Follow the steps on pages 10–11 that deal with preparing the planting area and digging the planting holes. Plant this garden in the spring, in sun to part shade, after the danger of frost is past. If you prefer to plant this garden in autumn, leave spaces for the Chilean jasmine, flowering tobacco, and regal lily and add them the following spring.

Step 3: Install the vines first, planting them about 6 inches away from the base of the arbor. If the clematis has long enough tendrils, push the tendrils through the support or trellis; this will encourage the vine to weave through the trellis or support as it climbs. You will need to periodically push new growth through the supports in the same manner. The wisteria vine will curl around the trellis in a twining habit; twine it by hand if it doesn't do this by itself at first. Plant the Chilean jasmine in containers, using pre-mixed potting soil or a homemade concoction of potting soil, perlite, and peat moss or a similar combination. After the containerized vines have had a few weeks to become established, add a granular perennial "starter" formula fertilizer to the soil.

Step 4: Next, plant the crabapple, then the shrubs and rosebushes. Place the tree or shrub into the planting hole on top of the loosened soil. Once the plant is level, straight, and centered in the hole, start filling in around the sides of the plant, using the soil set aside when the hole was dug. Once all the soil has been filled in, create a hollow in the soil around the trunk or base of the plant. This will direct water right to the root zone.

Prune out broken or diseased branches as you go. Work granular rose fertilizer pellets into the soil a few inches from the roots, using a hand fork. Do not fertilize the crabapple at all during the first year; remember that fertilizer is not always necessary and excessive fertilization of crabapples can encourage the growth of messy shoots and water sprouts.

Step 5: Plant the lilies to a depth of about 8 inches, about a foot apart, using a narrow-bladed hand trowel.

(The base of a lily bulb is more flat, and the top is slightly pointed.) Finally, install the hostas, evening primrose, and the flowering tobacco—the latter is usually sold by the flat or in 4- to 6-inch pots. Use a shovel or pitchfork to mulch around the newly planted trees and shrubs, but spread mulch by hand around annuals, perennials, and vines.

Step 6: Water the newly planted garden well. Water the new transplants carefully over a period of several weeks. Each plant should receive about an inch of water a week in its root zone. Use a soft spray attachment on the hose to prevent the soil from being washed away.

CALENDAR OF CARE

SPRING: *Prune back the rosebushes to a height of about 2 feet. Bring exotic vines outdoors in late spring if they have been overwintered indoors. Acclimatize them by setting them out for a few hours each day, bringing them in at night, for 3 to 4 days. This is a good time to repot container plants, if needed, adding a granular fertilizer. Plant annual flowering tobacco after the danger of frost is past.*

SUMMER: *Provide extra support for the vines, if necessary. Continue training new tendrils through the supports. Shear back the evening primrose, if necessary, and prune the shrubs when they have finished flowering. Fertilize the flowering tobacco and the rose bushes in June and July, but no later than that.*

AUTUMN: *Bring the containers of Chilean jasmine indoors for the cold months of autumn and winter. Let them stay a little dry and do not fertilize them. After the first frost, cut back all dead foliage of perennials. Prune back the shrubs to improve their shape, if desired. Prune all shoots from the base of the crabapple; remove crossed or broken branches and messy sprouts from the branches. Clean all blades carefully, especially after trimming diseased leaves or branches. Clean all tools and store them for the winter.*

WINTER: *After the ground has frozen, apply additional mulch (no more than 3 inches deep) to keep plant roots from heaving out of the soil as the weather goes through freeze and thaw cycles.*

GETTING TO KNOW THE PLANTS

1. CHILEAN JASMINE (*Mandevilla laxa*, formerly *M. suaveolens*)

CLASSIFICATION: Tender tropical vine, annual
PLANT HARDINESS ZONES: 9 to 10
ULTIMATE SIZE: To 15' tall
BLOOM TIME: Summer
SUN REQUIREMENT: Full sun

There is currently a craze for exotic flowers, and highly fragrant Chilean jasmine certainly fit the bill. Chilean jasmine should be grown in full sun and moist soil; this plan calls for it to be planted in a container and overwintered indoors or in a greenhouse. As beautiful and fragrant as this plant is, it may be hard to find. If that is the case, the white-flowered star jasmine (*Trachelospermum jasminoides*), a fragrant tropical plant, is a more readily available alternative.

CHILEAN JASMINE

2. HENRY CLEMATIS (*Clematis* x *henryii*)

CLASSIFICATION: Perennial vine
PLANT HARDINESS ZONES: 4 to 8
ULTIMATE SIZE: To about 5' tall
BLOOM TIME: Late spring to early summer
SUN REQUIREMENT: Full sun with shade or protection for roots

Large-flowering clematis vines have delicate foliage and thin, brittle stems that need the support of a fence, arbor, or trellis. 'Henryii' is well-known and easy to find, and its flowers are outstanding—8 inches across and pure white with ornamental stamens. After flowering, the remaining seedheads are attractive, too. The only trick to growing clematis is to keep the foliage and flowers in sun while keeping the roots in cool shade. This sounds complicated but is as easy as planting a dense but shallow-rooted groundcover around the base of the vine, underplanting with foliage plants that will shade the roots, or simply shading the roots with a garden ornament such as a large urn or birdbath.

HENRY CLEMATIS

3. WHITE CHINESE WISTERIA (*Wisteria sinensis* 'Alba')

CLASSIFICATION: Perennial vine
PLANT HARDINESS ZONES: 5/6 to 9
ULTIMATE SIZE: To 40' tall
BLOOM TIME: Late spring to early summer
SUN REQUIREMENT: Full sun to part shade

'Alba' is a white-flowering form of Chinese wisteria, which usually produces blue-violet flowers. Both forms produce huge, drooping racemes of flowers up to a foot long. Unless you are purchasing a large, established, and no doubt expensive wisteria plant, be prepared to wait several years for it to flower. Fertilize the plant when it is young to promote growth but not once it has become established. Many people make the mistake of planting a small wisteria plant propped against a lightweight trellis. This vine gets woody and very heavy as it matures and it requires extremely sturdy supports—steel, sturdy wood, iron, even concrete would not be out of line as materials for a pergola or arbor.

A SUBSTITUTE
If you don't want to make the investment a sturdy trellis requires, or if you live in the South, where wisteria grows very fast and can be invasive, plant *Clematis montana* 'Rubens', a delicate-looking, fragrant vine.

WHITE CHINESE WISTERIA

KOREANSPICE VIBURNUM

4. KOREANSPICE VIBURNUM (*Viburnum carlesii*)

CLASSIFICATION: Ornamental shrub
PLANT HARDINESS ZONES: 4 to 7
ULTIMATE SIZE: To 5' tall (occasionally much taller) and somewhat wider
BLOOM TIME: Mid- to late spring
SUN REQUIREMENT: Sun to part shade

The beautiful flowers of Koreanspice viburnum would be reason enough to plant this hardy shrub, but it is also favored with the most wonderful fragrance. Judd viburnum (*Viburnum* x *juddii*) is a newer hybrid that some prefer to Koreanspice viburnum; both have ornamental flowers and spectacular fragrance, so you won't go wrong with either one. Both Judd and Koreanspice viburnums perform equally well in full sun to part shade; just be sure to plant them near a path or a window where their fragrance can be enjoyed to the fullest.

'BLANC DOUBLE DE COUBERT' HYBRID RUGOSA ROSE

5. 'BLANC DOUBLE DE COUBERT' HYBRID RUGOSA ROSE
(*Rosa* x 'Blanc Double de Coubert')

CLASSIFICATION: Hardy shrub rose
PLANT HARDINESS ZONES: 4 to 9
ULTIMATE SIZE: 5'–6' tall and wide
BLOOM TIME: Late spring to early summer
SUN REQUIREMENT: Full sun

'Blanc Double de Coubert' has a lot to offer—it is winter hardy, rarely affected by disease, and it even has some yellow autumn color. While most rugosa roses are winter hardy, this rose is exceptionally so. The moderate-sized flowers are profuse and very fragrant, with a strong first bloom and limited reblooming. It is possible to increase the repeat bloom by deadheading the flowers, but if you can put up with the dead flowerheads you will be repaid with colorful rosehips in the autumn. Although 'Blanc Double de Coubert' can get rather large, it easily controlled by pruning. Roses perform best when they are planted in full sun, and fertilized and watered regularly. The roots of hardy shrub roses should be mulched to keep out weeds, but they require little other winter protection.

6. VARIEGATED SWEET MOCK ORANGE   (*Philadelphus coronarius* 'Variegatus')

CLASSIFICATION: Ornamental shrub
PLANT HARDINESS ZONES: 4 to 8
ULTIMATE SIZE: To about 10' tall and wide
BLOOM TIME: Late spring to early summer
SUN REQUIREMENT: Full sun to part shade

The variegated form of sweet mock orange has green leaves edged in creamy white; it is more ornamental than the species. The abundant white flowers have incomparable fragrance—cut a few flowering branches and bring them indoors, just like cut flowers. Plant sweet mock orange in full sun to part shade in moist, well-drained soil; prune back the branches after flowering.

VARIEGATED SWEET MOCK ORANGE

7. FLOWERING TOBACCO
(Nicotiana alata)

CLASSIFICATION: Annual
PLANT HARDINESS ZONES: 8 to 10
ULTIMATE SIZE: To 4' tall and 2' wide
BLOOM TIME: All summer
SUN REQUIREMENT: Part sun to part shade

The flower specified for this garden plan is the true, old-fashioned species of flowering tobacco, with none of the modern improvements. The original plant gets tall and a little floppy—don't stake them, though, just install lower growing plants in front of them to support the stems as they are weighed down by the abundant bloom. Flowering tobacco is extremely fragrant but only during the evening hours, which is perfect since this is a night-blooming annual. Plant it in part sun to part shade and keep the soil evenly moist.

FLOWERING TOBACCO

REGAL LILY

8. REGAL LILY *(Lilium regale)*

CLASSIFICATION: Hardy bulb
PLANT HARDINESS ZONES: 4 to 8
ULTIMATE SIZE: To 6' tall
BLOOM TIME: Summer
SUN REQUIREMENT: Sun to part shade

The blossoms of regal lily are beautiful and heavily fragrant; the plant is vigorous and will multiply freely. Despite its height, the regal lily is unlikely to ever need staking. They flower best when planted in full sun, but their roots like the protection of shade, and the soil should also be moist but very well drained. It is easy to shade the roots and lower stems of lilies by planting them at the middle or back of the border, where the foliage of other plants will shelter the base of the stem without blocking the sun from the bud or flower. Since lily stems leave something to be desired before and after flowering, this planting method serves a two-fold purpose.

TUFTED EVENING PRIMROSE

9. TUFTED EVENING PRIMROSE
(*Oenothera caespitosa*)

CLASSIFICATION: Native perennial
PLANT HARDINESS ZONES: 4 to 7
ULTIMATE SIZE: To 8" tall and 12" wide
BLOOM TIME: Early summer
SUN REQUIREMENT: Full sun to part shade

Tufted evening primrose begins to flower in late afternoon and continues flowering through the evening as its heady fragrance perfumes the night air. This is a very low-growing plant that becomes almost buried in fragrant white flowers that gradually fade to pink. Beware of selecting other pink-flowering forms of evening primrose because some are too invasive for a flower bed or border. Plant in full sun to part shade and keep the soil evenly moist.

10. 'PLANTAGINEA' HOSTA
(*Hosta plantaginea*, H. x 'Plantaginea')

CLASSIFICATION: Hardy perennial
PLANT HARDINESS ZONES: 3 to 8
ULTIMATE SIZE: Up to 18" tall and 24" wide
BLOOM TIME: Late summer
SUN REQUIREMENT: Part sun to shade

This exceptional hosta has shiny, light green leaves and a neat, mounded form but it is best known for its lily-shaped white flowers, which are very fragrant and twice the size of other hosta flowers. *H. plantaginea* is the only species of hosta that blooms at night—perfect for a moonlight garden. The flowers actually open in late afternoon, remaining open throughout the evening, when the fragrance is most pronounced. Fragrant hostas perform best in at least partial sun.

'PLANTAGINEA' HOSTA

11. 'SATIN CLOUD' CRABAPPLE
(*Malus* x 'Satin Cloud')

CLASSIFICATION: Compact ornamental tree
PLANT HARDINESS ZONES: 4 to 8
ULTIMATE SIZE: About 10' tall and wide
BLOOM TIME: Late spring to early summer
SUN REQUIREMENT: Full sun

This crabapple is exceptional in every way, starting with its exceptionally compact size and densely rounded form. The abundant flowers are large, pure white, and have a wonderful cinnamon-clove fragrance that is stronger on older trees. The thick green leaves turn a brilliant orange-red to purple in the autumn; the small fruits turn from a greenish yellow to a rich amber-yellow and are very persistent. Plant crabapples in full sun for best flowering and fruiting, in moist but well-drained soil.

'SATIN CLOUD' CRABAPPLE

LANDSCAPE LIGHTING

To make the most of an evening garden, use subtle lighting to enhance the garden without distracting from the flowers. Consider tiny white Christmas lights—sometimes called fairy lights—either strung through the trees, along a deck or fence railing, or attached to a trellis or arbor. If you have a pergola, so much the better, because the tiny lights look magical when strung among the structure and vines.

Torchlights are a wonderful addition, as long as they are kept at a safe distance from anything flammable. Japanese lanterns strung across the yard or garden add a festive touch, as do tiny votive candles massed along flat deck railings to create an alluring effect. For a safer way to display votive candles, look for interesting metal lanterns with cut-outs to reflect the light; hang these from iron hooks.

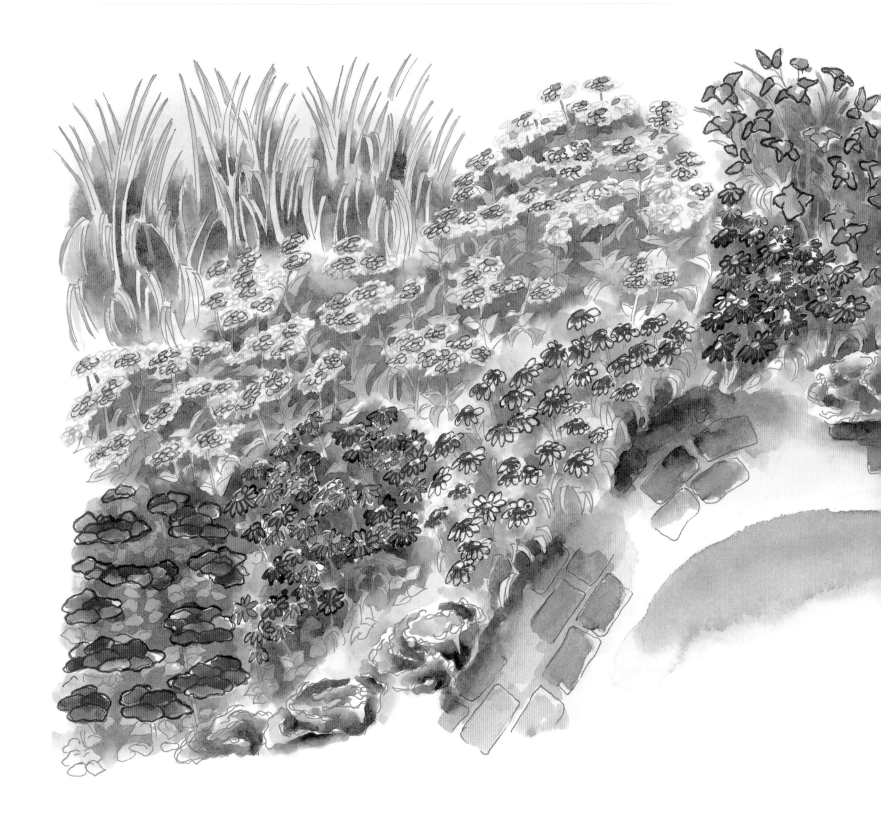

A LATE-SEASON COLOR GARDEN

By late summer, many annuals have passed their prime, and chrysanthemums appear by the millions. This garden was designed to add color and interest at a time when most gardens are in the doldrums. Because most of the plants require minimal care, this is an ideal design for a beginning gardener.

All of the plants in this garden can be planted in autumn, and will perform best in full sun and well-drained soil. Other than deadheading to promote repeat bloom and cutting back the dead foliage after frost, these plants will require little maintenance. Since all but the ornamental kale are hardy perennials and will return each year, they will grow into large clumps which may need to be divided into separate clumps of plants after three to five years. This is done by digging and "lifting" the whole clump out of the soil. Do not worry about root division unless the plants seem to be less vigorous or unless the centers of the plant appear to be fading, with new growth concentrated on the sides.

YOU WILL NEED...

- A square-ended spade if sod has to be removed

- A garden fork to loosen the soil

- A round-pointed shovel for planting any gallon-size or larger containers of perennials

- A broad-bladed hand trowel for planting smaller perennials

- A curved pruning saw for cutting back the grasses

- A wheelbarrow for moving soil, sod, plants, and debris

- Amendments to soil if needed or desired: peat moss, shredded leaves, sand, aged manure, or compost, for example

- Mulch, as needed, to spread to a depth of 3 inches around the plants when installed

- Pruning shears to cut away any dead, diseased, or damaged branches or flowers

- Garden gloves and garden shoes or boots

PLANT LIST

1. 'Morning Light' Japanese silver grass (*Miscanthus sinensis* 'Morning Light')

2. 'Summer Sun' false sunflower (*Heliopsis helianthoides* 'Summer Sun')

3. 'Goblin' blanket flower (*Gaillardia* x *grandiflora* 'Goblin')

4. 'Moorheim Beauty' sneezeweed (*Helenium autumnale* 'Moorheim Beauty')

5. Ornamental kale (*Brassica oleracea*)

6. 'Autumn Joy' sedum (*Sedum* x 'Autumn Joy', syn. *Hylotelephium* x 'Autumn Joy')

7. 'Goldsturm' black-eyed Susan (*Rudbeckia fulgida* var. *sullivantii* 'Goldsturm')

8. 'Indian Paintbrush' daylily (*Hemerocallis* x 'Indian Paintbrush')

A LATE-SEASON COLOR GARDEN

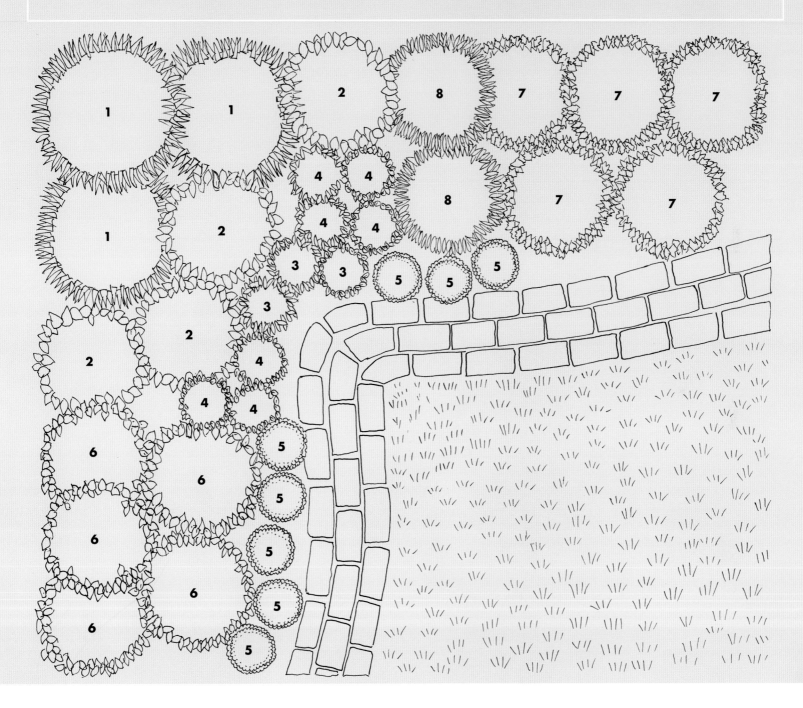

PLANTING THE LATE-SEASON COLOR GARDEN, STEP BY STEP

Step 1: Follow the steps on pages 10–11 that explain how to prepare the planting area and dig the planting holes. This garden can be planted in spring or autumn, in full sun. If installing the garden in the autumn, wait until spring to plant the ornamental kale, since it is marginally hardy, or substitute hardy chrysanthemums.

Step 2: Plant the ornamental grasses first, making sure to allow enough space (about 4 feet) for their ultimate width. Do not stint on this space, because grasses tend to reach their mature size very quickly, and they are easier to plant than to remove.

Step 3: Install the plants at the back of the border first—the 'Autumn Joy' sedum, false sunflower, daylily, and black-eyed Susan. Apply mulch and remove broken branches or foliage as you go. Many of the perennials in this plan become fairly large when mature; check the mature size of the plants as detailed in "Getting to Know the Plants," and leave sufficient space between plants.

Step 4: Next, plant the remaining flowers and foliage plants—blanket flower, sneezeweed, and ornamental kale—again working from the back to the front.

Step 5: Water the plants well. Some gardeners seem to think that once autumn arrives, the hoses can be packed away. Not so—plants that are installed in late summer or autumn need regularly watering for several weeks, and the rain can not be depended on to fall in precise or regular amounts.

CALENDAR OF CARE

SPRING: *The ornamental kale can be planted in late spring, if you prefer. Cut back the Japanese silver grass with a folding saw to keep it looking neat. Fertilize perennials if you choose, but it may not be necessary. Remove winter mulch from the base of plants, but reapply mulch within the planting area. Pull out weeds as they emerge.*

SUMMER: *Deadhead the black-eyed Susans, the sneezeweed, blanket flower, and false sunflower to encourage repeat bloom. Fertilize until mid-July if needed. Remove weeds regularly.*

AUTUMN: *After the first frost, cut back all dead foliage; dispose of undiseased plant waste in a compost heap. Destroy diseased plant remains so they don't contaminate other plants. Prune back the shrubs to improve their shape, if desired. Clean blades carefully, especially after trimming diseased leaves or branches.*

WINTER: *After the ground has frozen, apply additional mulch (no more than 3 inches deep) to keep plant roots from heaving out of the soil as the weather goes through freeze and thaw cycles.*

GETTING TO KNOW THE PLANTS

'MORNING LIGHT' JAPANESE SILVER GRASS

1. 'MORNING LIGHT' JAPANESE SILVER GRASS (*Miscanthus sinensis* 'Morning Light', syn. 'Gracillimus Variegatus')

CLASSIFICATION: Ornamental grass
PLANT HARDINESS ZONES: 5 to 9
ULTIMATE SIZE: To 5' tall, slightly less wide
BLOOM TIME: Late summer to autumn
SUN REQUIREMENT: Full sun

The green and white leaves of 'Morning Light' Japanese silver grass are very attractive in color and form, and the feathery flowers late in the season are an added bonus. When this grass goes dormant in the winter, the foliage fades to a dark tan and the flowers turn a creamy ivory, but both hold up well even in harsh winters. To keep this grass looking neat, scythe it down to about 1 or 2 feet in early spring. Japanese silver grass grows quickly into a dense plant that blows in the breeze.

A WARM-CLIMATE ALTERNATIVE
In warmer climates, where *Miscanthus* species can cause problems with their self-sowing seeds, the less hardy white-flowering fountain grass (*Pennisetum caudatum*) may be a better alternative.

2. 'SUMMER SUN' FALSE SUNFLOWER, OXEYE DAISY
(*Heliopsis helianthoides* 'Summer Sun')

CLASSIFICATION: Perennial
PLANT HARDINESS ZONES: 3 to 9
ULTIMATE SIZE: To 4' tall and wide
BLOOM TIME: Summer to autumn
SUN REQUIREMENT: Sun to part shade

This easy-to-grow perennial lights up the garden for months on end, as the flowers just keep on blooming. Although 'Summer Sun' is a daisy-type flower, its petals are just a shade or two lighter than its central golden disk. While 'Summer Sun' gets to be quite tall, the sturdy stems do not usually require staking. Deadheading the flowers will increase the repeat bloom.

OTHER GOOD CULTIVARS
Other excellent false sunflower cultivars include:
'Light of Loddon' • 'Goldgreenheart' • 'Golden Plume'

'SUMMER SUN' FALSE SUNFLOWER

'GOBLIN' BLANKET FLOWER

3. 'GOBLIN' BLANKET FLOWER
(*Gaillardia* x *grandiflora* 'Goblin')

CLASSIFICATION: Perennial
PLANT HARDINESS ZONES: 2 to 10
ULTIMATE SIZE: To 12" tall and wide
BLOOM TIME: All summer
SUN REQUIREMENT: Full sun

Blanket flower is an undemanding, heat-loving perennial valued for its brilliantly colored flowers and its long period of bloom. 'Goblin' is a neatly compact form that can be used equally well at the front of the border or in a mixed perennial bed; it will survive a variety of soil conditions but performs best in full sun.

'MOORHEIM BEAUTY' SNEEZEWEED

4. 'MOORHEIM BEAUTY' SNEEZEWEED
(*Helenium autumnale* 'Moorheim Beauty')

CLASSIFICATION: Perennial
PLANT HARDINESS ZONES: 3 to 8
ULTIMATE SIZE: To 4' tall and wide
BLOOM TIME: Mid- to late summer through autumn
SUN REQUIREMENT: Full sun

'Moorheim Beauty' blooms in a rich tapestry of gold, rust, red, brown, and bronze—the flowers have a dark brown center and rust to red-brown petals edged with a fine border of gold. Sneezeweed has strong stems that do not normally require staking even when they get quite tall.

OTHER RECOMMENDED CULTIVARS
'Crimson Beauty' • 'Riverton Beauty' • 'Butterpat' • 'Brilliant' • 'Wyndley' • 'The Bishop' • 'Coppelia'

5. ORNAMENTAL KALE, ORNAMENTAL CABBAGE
(*Brassica oleracea*)

CLASSIFICATION: Annual
PLANT HARDINESS ZONES: 7 to 10
ULTIMATE SIZE: To 18" tall and wide
BLOOM TIME: Ornamental midsummer through autumn
SUN REQUIREMENT: Sun to part shade

The neat, rounded mounds of ornamental kale make it a useful edging plant, since it starts to look good from the moment the green shoots emerge from the ground. The foliage color is best when planted in full sun, but ornamental kale will also hold up in partial shade. In mild winters, it may survive the season but it tends to get straggly with age.

ORNAMENTAL KALE

6. 'AUTUMN JOY' SEDUM   (Sedum x 'Autumn Joy', syn. *Hylotelephium* x 'Autumn Joy', sometimes listed as *Hylotelephium spectabile*)

CLASSIFICATION: Hardy hybrid perennial
PLANT HARDINESS ZONES: 3 to 8
ULTIMATE SIZE: About 24" tall and 18"–24" wide
BLOOM TIME: Form in spring; "bloom" in brighter colors starting in late summer
SUN REQUIREMENT: Sun to part shade

'Autumn Joy' sedum is exceptionally dependable, making it an excellent choice for beginning gardeners. The sturdy, succulent foliage is attractive from early spring through autumn, with color-changing flowers providing an added attraction. 'Autumn Joy' retains its form through the winter; if you like the brown winter foliage, cut back the dead foliage in spring. If not, cut it back after the first hard frost. Although this plant was recently reclassified into the genus *Hylotelephium*, most garden centers continue to label it *Sedum* x 'Autumn Joy'.

'AUTUMN JOY' SEDUM

'GOLDSTURM' BLACK-EYED SUSAN

7. 'GOLDSTURM' BLACK-EYED SUSAN
(*Rudbeckia fulgida* var. *sullivantii* 'Goldsturm')

CLASSIFICATION: Perennial
PLANT HARDINESS ZONES: 3 to 10
ULTIMATE SIZE: About 2' tall and wide
BLOOM TIME: Midsummer through autumn
SUN REQUIREMENT: Full sun

Black-eyed Susan is a common name that has been applied to quite a few plants, and in this case it should really be "brown-eyed Susan." The cultivar 'Goldsturm' identifies one of the best forms of this excellent and carefree perennial (watch out for plants marked "Goldsturm Strain" which is not quite the same thing). 'Goldsturm' earned its reputation because it requires little maintenance yet produces huge quantities of flowers that bloom for weeks on end.

8. 'INDIAN PAINTBRUSH' DAYLILY

(*Hemerocallis* x 'Indian Paintbrush')

CLASSIFICATION: Hardy perennial
PLANT HARDINESS ZONES: 3 to 9
ULTIMATE SIZE: To about 30" tall
BLOOM TIME: Midsummer
SUN REQUIREMENT: Full sun

Daylilies are very easy to grow and they multiply nicely without getting out of bounds. The flowers last only a day, but new flowers bloom continually. The warm colors of 'Indian Paintbrush' look great with the autumn colors in this plan; other red, wine, or deep gold daylilies would also work if 'Indian Paintbrush' proves hard to find. Plant daylilies in a sunny spot and water until they become established; you will be rewarded with a steady parade of fantastic flowers.

'INDIAN PAINTBRUSH' DAYLILY

MORE AUTUMN FLOWERS

Mums are great, but there are many other wonderful plants that can make an autumn garden something to get excited about. The following plants all bloom or rebloom in autumn—try to make room for a few of these lesser-used perennials to give the garden some zip before the frost zaps it.

Asters (*Aster* spp.) • Daisy fleabane (*Erigeron speciosus*) • Gaura (*Gaura lindheimerei*) • Himalayan fleeceflower (*Polygonum bistorta* 'Superbum') • Japanese anemone (*Anemone* x *hybrida*) • Joe-Pye weed (*Eupatorium* spp.) • Obedient plant (*Phystostegia virginiana*) • Perennial sunflower (*Helianthus* x *multiflora*) • Russian sage (*Perovskia atriplicifolia*) • Speedwell (*Veronica* spp.) • Starflower (*Boltonia asteroides*) • Stoke's aster (*Stokesia* spp.) • Wormwood (*Artemisia* spp.)

A SHADY DECK OR PATIO GARDEN

While this garden was designed for a somewhat basic rectangular deck or patio, it can easily be adapted to fit decks or patios that have a different shape or layout of steps and entrances. For townhouses or ground-floor condos with decks or patios and little space, pick one section of the plan and modify it to fit your existing garden area.

Since this is primarily a garden for spring and early summer, you may want to add containers of shade-loving annuals such as begonias or impatiens (see Annuals for Shady Spots on page 123 for suggestions), followed by containers of chrysanthemums, to provide color in the late summer and autumn. Mums prefer full sun but as long as there is at least partial sun they should do just fine.

YOU WILL NEED...

- A square-ended spade if sod has to be removed

- A garden fork to loosen the soil

- A round-pointed shovel for planting the magnolia and shrubs, as well as any gallon-size or larger containers of perennials

- A broad-bladed hand trowel for planting smaller perennials, if needed

- A wheelbarrow for moving soil, sod, plants, and debris

- Amendments to soil if needed or desired: peat moss, shredded leaves, sand, aged manure, or compost, for example

- Mulch, as needed, to spread to a depth of 3 inches around the plants when installed

- Pruning shears to cut away any dead, diseased, or damaged branches or flowers

- Garden gloves and garden shoes or boots

PLANT LIST

1. Star magnolia (*Magnolia stellata*)

2. Oakleaf hydrangea (*Hydrangea quercifolia*)

3. 'Hahs' American cranberrybush viburnum (*Viburnum trilobum* 'Hahs')

4. 'Frances Williams' hosta (*Hosta* x 'Frances Williams')

5. 'Zounds' hosta (*Hosta* x 'Zounds')

6. Bleeding heart (*Dicentra spectabilis*)

7. Lady's mantle (*Alchemilla mollis*)

8. 'Snow Queen' columbine (*Aquilegia* x 'Snow Queen')

9. 'Peach Blossom' astilbe (*Astilbe* x *rosea* 'Peach Blossom')

A SHADY DECK OR PATIO GARDEN

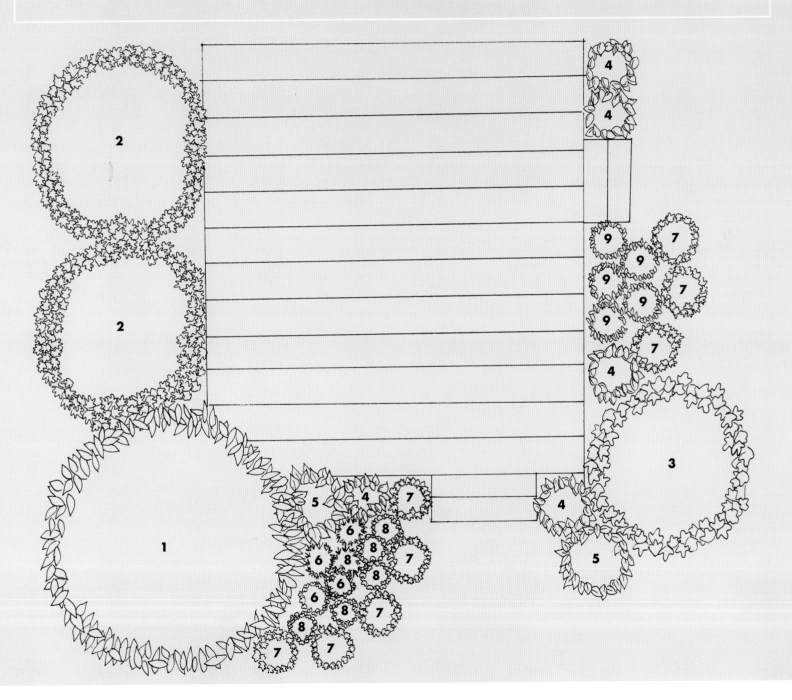

PLANTING THE SHADY DECK OR PATIO GARDEN, STEP BY STEP

Step 1: Install this garden around an existing deck or patio. Follow the steps on pages 10–11 that explain how to prepare the planting area and dig the planting holes. This garden can be planted in spring or autumn, in part sun to part shade.

Step 2: Plant the star magnolia first, placing the tree into the planting hole on top of the loosened soil. Once the plant is level, straight, and centered in the hole, start filling in around the sides of the plant, using the soil you set aside while digging the hole. Give the magnolia plenty of room to grow—it is an ornamental tree, but it is still a tree.

Step 3: Next, install the shrubs—the oakleaf hydrangea and the American cranberrybush viburnum, giving them sufficient room to grow (see "Getting to Know the Plants" to verify their mature size). Remove any dead or diseased branches, and spread the mulch around these as you go. Be sure to remove any weeds or stones from the soil, too.

Step 4: Plant the hostas, then the remaining perennials (the bleeding heart, lady's mantle, columbine, and astilbe), working from the back of the garden space to the front. Remove any broken or damaged foliage and prune away any broken roots. Apply mulch using a scoop shovel or pitchfork around the trees and shrubs, but spread the mulch by hand around the perennials.

Step 5: Water the garden well after all the plants have been installed. Water the new transplants carefully over a period of several weeks. Each plant should receive about an inch of water a week in its root zone.

CALENDAR OF CARE

SPRING: *Remove winter mulch from around the base of plants, reapplying mulch to the planting area. Keep plants watered as they emerge, and fertilize if necessary (but do not fertilize the trees and shrubs during the first year). Remove weeds as they appear.*

SUMMER: *Cut back the foliage of the bleeding heart if it becomes unsightly. Remove dead flowers from the hostas, false spirea, and lady's mantle as needed. Remove weeds regularly and water. Prune the shrubs in late summer or autumn, when they have finished flowering.*

AUTUMN: *After the first frost, cut back all dead foliage; dispose of undiseased plant waste in a compost heap. Destroy diseased plant remains so they don't contaminate other plants. Prune back the shrubs to improve their shape, if desired. Clean blades carefully, especially after trimming diseased leaves or branches.*

WINTER: *After the ground has frozen, apply additional mulch (no more than 3 inches deep) to keep plant roots from heaving out of the soil as the weather goes through freeze and thaw cycles.*

GETTING TO KNOW THE PLANTS

STAR MAGNOLIA

1. STAR MAGNOLIA (*Magnolia stellata*)

CLASSIFICATION: Large shrub or small tree
PLANT HARDINESS ZONES: 4 to 8
ULTIMATE SIZE: To 20' tall and 15' wide
BLOOM TIME: Spring
SUN REQUIREMENT: Full sun to light shade

Star magnolia's fragrant flowers unfurl like masses of white stars; this ornamental shrub has clean, dark green foliage that looks great even when the tree is not in bloom. The risk with the early-blooming magnolia is that the buds and blossoms may be destroyed by frost if they open too soon. To guard against this, do not plant magnolias in a southern exposure; it also helps to site magnolias where they will have some protection—under taller trees or in a corner where fences or walls offer shelter. Plant in full sun to part shade in soil that is evenly moist and rich in organic matter.

2. OAKLEAF HYDRANGEA (*Hydrangea quercifolia*)

CLASSIFICATION: Ornamental shrub
PLANT HARDINESS ZONES: 5 to 9
ULTIMATE SIZE: To 6' tall and 8' wide, spreading
BLOOM TIME: Summer to autumn
SUN REQUIREMENT: Sun to part shade

As its name suggests, this hydrangea's large, deep green lobed leaves are reminiscent of oak leaves. They are a wonderful source of autumn color, turning red, rust, burgundy, and purple. The flowers are huge creamy white panicles, up to a foot long, that gradually turn pink to burgundy to dark red to brown. Although the shrub itself will survive fairly cold winters, the flower buds are vulnerable to extreme cold. This is a fast-growing, suckering shrub that will quickly fill in, so don't plant them too close together.

RECOMMENDED CULTIVARS
'Snow Queen' • 'PeeWee' • 'Snowflake'

OAKLEAF HYDRANGEA

3. 'HAHS' AMERICAN CRANBERRYBUSH VIBURNUM

(*Viburnum trilobum* 'Hahs')

CLASSIFICATION: Ornamental shrub
PLANT HARDINESS ZONES: 2 to 7
ULTIMATE SIZE: To 12' tall and wide
BLOOM TIME: Late spring
SUN REQUIREMENT: Sun to part shade

This reliable native shrub has medium green foliage that is attractive in summer but outstanding in the autumn, when it turns yellow to red to purple. The creamy white flowers are ornamental in the spring and the bright red berries add another dimension of interest in autumn and early winter. 'Hahs' is a compact form with large red fruits. It is undemanding and performs well in sun to part shade, provided that the soil is well-drained and kept evenly moist.

'HAHS' AMERICAN CRANBERRYBUSH VIBURNUM

'FRANCES WILLIAMS' HOSTA

4. 'FRANCES WILLIAMS' HOSTA

(*Hosta* x 'Frances Williams', syn.
H. sieboldiana 'Frances Williams')

CLASSIFICATION: Hardy perennial
PLANT HARDINESS ZONES: 3 to 8
ULTIMATE SIZE: To 22" tall and 48" wide
BLOOM TIME: Summer
SUN REQUIREMENT: Part sun to shade

'Frances Williams' is consistently one of the top ten most popular hostas in American Hosta Society polls. It has leaves up to 13 inches long and 11 inches wide The thick foliage is a deep blue-green edged with creamy yellow margins, but the color may fade if the plant is exposed to too much sunlight.

'ZOUNDS' HOSTA

5. 'ZOUNDS' HOSTA   (*Hosta* x 'Zounds')

CLASSIFICATION: Hardy perennial
PLANT HARDINESS ZONES: **3 to 8**
ULTIMATE SIZE: To 16" tall and 30" wide
BLOOM TIME: Summer
SUN REQUIREMENT: Part sun to shade

This gold hosta is a hybrid of the well-known *Hosta sieboldiana* 'Elegans', and it shares the large, sturdy leaves of the parent plant. The individual leaves may reach 11 inches long and 8 or 9 inches wide. The leaves are thick and deeply ridged, which gives them the famous "seersucker" effect; the foliage has a glowing golden metallic sheen that is especially noticeable in the evening. 'Zounds' is also more slug-resistant than many cultivars.

6. BLEEDING HEART
(*Dicentra spectabilis*)

CLASSIFICATION: Hardy perennial
PLANT HARDINESS ZONES: **3 to 8**
ULTIMATE SIZE: To 3' high and 1¹/₂' wide
BLOOM TIME: Spring
SUN REQUIREMENT: Part sun to part shade

Common bleeding heart boasts sensational pink and white flowers in spring and delicate, attractive foliage. The only drawback is that it goes dormant and seems to disappear later in the season, which is why it is featured in this plan with large-leaved hostas, which will hide the fading bleeding heart. Don't be fooled into thinking the plants are dead, though—come spring, they will be back. Bleeding heart requires well-drained soil and will not survive "wet feet."

BLEEDING HEART

7. LADY'S MANTLE (*Alchemilla mollis*)

CLASSIFICATION: Hardy perennial
PLANT HARDINESS ZONES: 3 to 8
ULTIMATE SIZE: To 2' tall and 1½' wide
BLOOM TIME: Mid- to late summer
SUN REQUIREMENT: Part sun to part shade

Lady's mantle is a beautiful and very useful plant for gardens that are at least partially shaded and kept evenly moist. The frothy sprays of chartreuse flowers are ornamental and brighten a shady spot, but many gardeners feel the foliage of lady's mantle can stand alone without flowering at all. The neat mounds of green leaves are at their best after a light rain or in the morning dew when drops of water collect in the leaves.

LADY'S MANTLE

'SNOW QUEEN' COLUMBINE

8. 'SNOW QUEEN' COLUMBINE

(*Aquilegia* x 'Snow Queen')

CLASSIFICATION: Hardy perennial
PLANT HARDINESS ZONES: 5 to 9
ULTIMATE SIZE: To 3' tall and 1½' wide
BLOOM TIME: Spring to early summer
SUN REQUIREMENT: Part sun to part shade

Columbines are beautiful, old-fashioned flowers with attractive foliage and ornamental spring flowers. 'Snow Queen' and the similar hybrid 'Crystal' (sometimes known as 'Kristall') feature large white flowers that are beautiful when massed in a shady spot. They are compact plants that tend to bloom over a long period and work well in designs with other shade plants. Like bleeding heart, columbines tend to fade out after they have bloomed; by surrounding them with strong foliage plants the garden will keep a neater appearance throughout the summer. Columbine performs best in at least partial shade, where the soil is evenly moist but well drained.

'PEACH BLOSSOM' ASTILBE

9. 'PEACH BLOSSOM' ASTILBE, FALSE SPIREA
(*Astilbe* x *rosea* 'Peach Blossom', sometimes listed as *A.* x *arendsii* 'Peach Blossom')

CLASSIFICATION: Hardy perennial
PLANT HARDINESS ZONES: 4 to 8
ULTIMATE SIZE: About 2' tall and wide
BLOOM TIME: Early to midsummer
SUN REQUIREMENT: Best in part sun to part shade

Astilbe is a wonderful plant for the shade garden, and 'Peach Blossom' is just one of many hybrids available. The foliage is delicate and looks good even when the plants are not in bloom, but the feathery plumes of flowers—especially when massed—are hard to beat. Astilbe will not tolerate drought but neither will it tolerate wet feet; plant it in well-drained soil and keep it watered during the hot summer months. It responds well to an autumn application of fertilizer with a high ratio of nitrogen.

OTHER ASTILBE CULTIVARS
Some of the best cultivars include:
'Amethyst'—hot purple-pink • 'Bressingham Beauty'—deep pink • 'Cattleya'—rosy pink • 'Deutschland'—white • 'Fanal'—red • 'Montgomery'—dark red • 'Rheinland'—deep rose

CUSTOMIZE THIS PLAN FOR A SUNNY SPACE

The plants in the featured plan are best suited for a garden in partial shade, but you can substitute sun-loving plants if that better suits your space. Use the following plants in place of those in the featured plant list.

1. Star magnolia—Keep, or replace with the low but wide-growing Sargent crabapple (*Malus sargentii*)

2. 'Miss Kim' lilac (*Syringa patula* 'Miss Kim')—Instead of the oakleaf hydrangea

3. American cranberrybush viburnum—Keep, as in featured plan

4. 'Autumn Joy' sedum (*Sedum* x 'Autumn Joy' syn. *Hylotelephium* x 'Autumn Joy')

5. 'Heavy Metal' switch grass (*Panicum virgatum* 'Heavy Metal')

6. 'Crater Lake Blue' speedwell (*Veronica latifolia* 'Crater Lake Blue')

7. 'Moonbeam' threadleaf coreopsis (*Coreopsis verticillata* 'Moonbeam')

8. 'Alaska' shasta daisies (*Leucanthemum* x *superbum*, syn. *Chrysanthemum* x *superbum*)

9. 'Stella de Oro' daylily (*Hemerocallis* x 'Stella de Oro')

ANNUALS FOR SHADY SPOTS

Some gardeners assume that all annuals require full sun, but many perform better in at least partial shade. Following are some that will flourish in lightly shady spots.

Amethyst flower (*Browallia speciosa*)

Baby blue-eyes (*Nemophilia menziesii*)

Coleus (*Coleus*, syn. *Solenostemon*, spp.)

Dahlias (*Dahlia* spp.)

Edging lobelia (*Lobelia erinus*)

Flowering tobacco (*Nicotiana alata*)

Hybrid wax begonias (*Begonia* x *semperflorens-cultorum*)

Impatiens (*Impatiens wallerana*)

Madagascar periwinkle (*Catharanthus roseus*)

Mignonette (*Reseda odorata*)

Monkey flower (*Mimulus* spp.)

Pinks (*Dianthus* spp.)

Primrose (*Primula* x *polyantha*)

Stocks (*Matthiola* spp.)

Wallflowers (*Cheiranthus cheiri*, syn. *Erysimium cheiri*)

A BUTTERFLY GARDEN

The design of this garden can be altered to fit different shapes or sizes—its main purpose is to attract butterflies and add color to the landscape. The butterfly bush can be purchased as a small plant or as a larger shrub; it will attract more butterflies if you plant a shrub-sized plant at the outset.

The cosmos and zinnias can be purchased by the flat, but it is easier and cheaper to plant seeds directly into the soil. Cosmos will self-seed and come back year after year, but zinnias usually need to be replanted each spring. Sweet alyssum is usually sold by the flat, and that is probably the best way to plant it in this garden. Marjoram is sold in small pots but the aster, catmint, and milkweed should be purchased in 1-gallon containers if possible, to help the garden fill in quickly.

These are low-maintenance plants that can be fertilized if desired, but note that over-fertilizing will produce lush foliage at the expense of flowers.

You Will Need...

- A square-ended spade if sod has to be removed

- A garden fork to loosen the soil

- A level-headed rake for planting seeds

- A round-pointed shovel for planting any gallon-size or larger containers of perennials

- A broad-bladed hand trowel for planting smaller perennials

- A narrow-bladed hand trowel for planting flats

- A wheelbarrow for moving soil, sod, plants, and debris

- Amendments to soil if needed or desired: peat moss, shredded leaves, sand, aged manure, or compost, for example

- Mulch, as needed, to spread to a depth of 3 inches around the plants when installed

- Pea gravel for paths and a few flat rocks for the butterfly habitat

- A birdbath or other water feature to benefit the butterflies

- Pruning shears to cut away any dead, diseased, or damaged branches or flowers

- Garden gloves and garden shoes or boots

- Optional: A small salt lick for the butterflies

Plant List

1. Sweet marjoram (*Origanum majorana*)

2. 'Black Knight' butterfly bush (*Buddleia davidii* 'Black Knight')

3. 'Purple Dome' New England aster (*Aster novae-angliae* 'Purple Dome')

4. 'Blue Wonder' catmint (*Nepeta mussinii* 'Blue Wonder')

5. 'Sensation' cosmos (*Cosmos bipinnatus* 'Sensation')

6. 'Ruffled Mix' zinnia (*Zinnia elegans* 'Ruffled Mix')

7. Sweet alyssum (*Lobularia maritima*)

8. Swamp milkweed (*Asclepias incarnata*)

A BUTTERFLY GARDEN

PLANTING THE BUTTERFLY GARDEN, STEP BY STEP

Step 1: Install paths. A simple method is to mark out the path and remove the sod and about 6 inches of topsoil. Add a base of about 2 to 3 inches of construction sand, topped with 3 to 4 inches of wood chips, pea gravel, or slabs of flagstone. If you choose flagstone, brush sand or crushed gravel over and around each stone to ensure a tight fit. (Both flat stones and small pebbles are attractive and useful things to have in a butterfly habitat.)

Step 2: Follow the steps on pages 10–11 that explain how to prepare the planting area and dig the planting holes. Plant this garden in the spring, after danger of frost is past, in a site that gets full sun.

Step 3: Put larger garden accents or ornaments in place before installing any of the plants. Be sure that the ornament is firmly in position, so that it does not tip and injure a person or your plants.

Step 4: Plant the butterfly bushes first, placing the shrub in the planting hole on top of the loosened soil. Once the plant is level, straight, and centered in the hole, start filling in around the sides of the plant, using the soil set aside as holes were dug. Once all the soil has been filled in, create a hollow in the soil around the trunk or base of the plant. This will direct water right to the root zone.

Step 5: Next, plant the herbs and annuals, working outward from the base of the garden ornament and the shrubs. If you are planting annuals from seed, sow the seeds directly into the soil as soon as the danger of frost is past. Be sure to include some pebbles as mulch—around the milkweed would be best, since that plant loves water—and add sufficient water to make puddles for the butterflies. Do not clean up or weed this garden as often as you would other types of gardens, since some butterflies use weeds such as thistle for laying eggs, and others lay their eggs in piles of herbaceous or woody debris.

CALENDAR OF CARE

SPRING: *Plant seeds and annuals after the danger of frost is past. Pull up weeds as they appear—never use herbicides in a butterfly garden. Apply new mulch as needed. Keep plants watered and keep a supply of wet, muddy stones for the butterflies.*

SUMMER: *Pinch back the asters and catmint in early summer to promote a neat, bushy habit. Take cuttings from the marjoram for kitchen use or to dry for the winter. Shear the sweet alyssum with clippers to encourage repeat blooming and to form a dense, very low hedge. Remove dead flowers as needed and continue to water regularly.*

AUTUMN: *After the first frost, cut back dead foliage of all perennials and pull up dead annuals by the roots; dispose of undiseased plant waste in a compost heap. Destroy diseased plant remains so they don't contaminate other plants. Prune back the butterfly bush to about 12 to 18 inches. Clean blades carefully, especially after trimming diseased leaves or branches.*

WINTER: *After the ground has frozen, apply additional mulch (no more than 3 inches deep) to keep plant roots from heaving out of the soil as the weather goes through freeze and thaw cycles.*

BUTTERFLY ATTRACTORS

A large, complicated garden design is not essential to attract butterflies; they need only the basics of food, water, and shelter. Here are some proven butterfly favorites:

* Colorful flowers
* Nectar-producing plants
* Plants or structures that provide shelter (you can buy specially designed butterfly shelters)
* Water, particularly with nearby rocks for the butterflies to perch on
* Hot, sunny spots with some protection from the wind
* Deer licks
* Areas with plants growing at different heights

GETTING TO KNOW THE PLANTS

SWEET MARJORAM

1. SWEET MARJORAM
(*Origanum majorana*)

CLASSIFICATION: Tender perennial herb
PLANT HARDINESS ZONES: 6 to 9
ULTIMATE SIZE: To 2' tall, spreading
BLOOM TIME: Summer
SUN REQUIREMENT: Full sun

Sweet marjoram is not only useful for attracting butterflies, it also as a culinary herb. Its leaves are very aromatic with a flavor that is both sweeter and spicier than those of the related oregano. Plant it in full sun, in well-drained soil and where it has room to spread.

2. 'BLACK KNIGHT' BUTTERFLY BUSH
(*Buddleia davidii* 'Black Knight')

CLASSIFICATION: Ornamental shrub
PLANT HARDINESS ZONES: 5 to 9
ULTIMATE SIZE: To 10' tall and wide
BLOOM TIME: Early summer until frost
SUN REQUIREMENT: Full sun

This sprawling, heavily flowered shrub is well named because butterflies adore it. 'Black Knight' is a popular dark purple flowering form, but any butterfly bush will attract butterflies. Deadheading is a good idea—it encourages repeat bloom (and the dead flowers can become messy looking). Flowers are formed on new growth, so cut the shrub back to about 2 feet after flowering, which will keep it neat and also keep the size under control.

'BLACK NIGHT' BUTTERFLY BUSH

'PURPLE DOME' NEW ENGLAND ASTER

3. 'PURPLE DOME' NEW ENGLAND ASTER
(*Aster novae-angliae* 'Purple Dome')

CLASSIFICATION: Hardy perennial
PLANT HARDINESS ZONES: 4 to 9
ULTIMATE SIZE: To 2' tall and wide
BLOOM TIME: Autumn
SUN REQUIREMENT: Sun to part shade

The masses of purple flowers are stunning, and the compact form means that no staking is needed. Butterflies aren't particular about which aster you plant, so don't worry if you can't find the exact cultivar described here—there are hundreds of excellent asters to choose from. Do not overfertilize asters or plant them in overly rich soil.

4. 'BLUE WONDER' CATMINT, PERSIAN CATMINT
(*Nepeta mussinii* 'Blue Wonder')

CLASSIFICATION: Hardy perennial herb
PLANT HARDINESS ZONES: 3 to 8
ULTIMATE SIZE: To about 18" tall and wide
BLOOM TIME: All summer
SUN REQUIREMENT: Full sun

'Blue Wonder' catmint is sometimes used for edging because of its compact form. The gray-green foliage is a signal that this plant likes full sun and will tolerate dryness—many plants with similar foliage prefer these conditions. Shear catmint after flowering to keep it looking neat.

'BLUE WONDER' CATMINT

5. 'SENSATION' COSMOS
(*Cosmos bipinnatus* 'Sensation')

CLASSIFICATION: Annual
PLANT HARDINESS ZONES: 8 to 10
ULTIMATE SIZE: To 5'
BLOOM TIME: Midsummer to frost
SUN REQUIREMENT: Full sun, poor to average soil

Cosmos is one of the easiest annuals to grow, providing you don't pamper it. Too much fertilizer or too rich a soil, and you will have masses of foliage but few flowers. 'Sensation' is a tall form of cosmos with mixed colors of daisy-type flowers atop the feathery foliage. You can stake the taller types of cosmos or you can let them sprawl exuberantly over the lower plants in front of them, which act as supports. Cosmos will self-seed prolifically, so even after a hard winter some cosmos will pop up the following summer. Plant cosmos in full sun where it can bake in the heat, and water it occasionally—it is drought tolerant, heat tolerant, and long-blooming.

'SENSATION' COSMOS

'RUFFLED MIX' ZINNIA

6. 'RUFFLED MIX' ZINNIA
(*Zinnia elegans* 'Ruffled Mix')

CLASSIFICATION: Annual
PLANT HARDINESS ZONES: 8 to 10
ULTIMATE SIZE: To 3'
BLOOM TIME: All summer
SUN REQUIREMENT: Full sun

Zinnias are very easy to grow from seed, although it is sometimes possible to purchase them by the flat or in pots. 'Ruffles Mixed' is a suggested type of zinnia, but any colorful variety will work in this plan. Look for mildew-resistant, improved varieties since some of the older zinnias had a tendency to look shaggy by the end of summer; the newer ones don't suffer from this problem. Plant in full sun in average soil and water regularly until they are established.

7. SWEET ALYSSUM   (*Lobularia maritima*)

CLASSIFICATION: Annual
PLANT HARDINESS ZONES: 8 to 10
ULTIMATE SIZE: To 8"
BLOOM TIME: Late spring through summer
SUN REQUIREMENT: Sun to part shade

Once the danger of frost is past, sweet alyssum will grow easily from seed that is sown directly in the planting bed. It is also possible to purchase sweet alyssum by the pot or by the flat. While sweet alyssum performs best in full sun, it will also work well in planting areas that get some shade. For best results, keep the soil evenly moist.

OTHER GOOD CULTIVARS
'Carpet of Snow' • 'Rosie O'Day' • 'Royal Carpet' •
'Snow Crystals' • 'Sweet White'

SWEET ALYSSUM

SWAMP MILKWEED

8. SWAMP MILKWEED, SILKWEED   (*Asclepias incarnata*)

CLASSIFICATION: Native perennial herb
PLANT HARDINESS ZONES: 3 to 8
ULTIMATE SIZE: 2'–4' tall and 2' wide
BLOOM TIME: Summer
SUN REQUIREMENT: Sun to part shade

Swamp milkweed is related to the orange-flowering native butterfly weed (*Asclepias tuberosa*), both of which are attractive to butterflies. As the name indicates, swamp milkweed is native to swamps and marshes, so be sure to give it plenty of water. It prefers full sun but will also perform well in partial shade. Swamp milkweed can be planted by seed or as small potted plants, but avoid purchasing larger plants, which do not usually transplant well.

PLANT HARDINESS ZONES

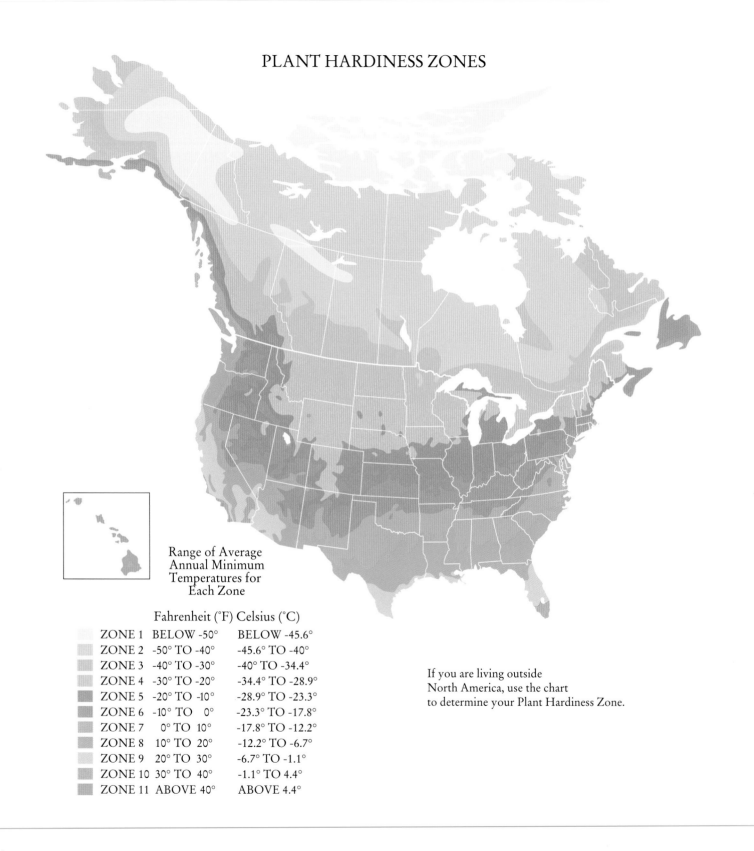

Range of Average
Annual Minimum
Temperatures for
Each Zone

		Fahrenheit (°F)	Celsius (°C)
	ZONE 1	BELOW -50°	BELOW -45.6°
	ZONE 2	-50° TO -40°	-45.6° TO -40°
	ZONE 3	-40° TO -30°	-40° TO -34.4°
	ZONE 4	-30° TO -20°	-34.4° TO -28.9°
	ZONE 5	-20° TO -10°	-28.9° TO -23.3°
	ZONE 6	-10° TO 0°	-23.3° TO -17.8°
	ZONE 7	0° TO 10°	-17.8° TO -12.2°
	ZONE 8	10° TO 20°	-12.2° TO -6.7°
	ZONE 9	20° TO 30°	-6.7° TO -1.1°
	ZONE 10	30° TO 40°	-1.1° TO 4.4°
	ZONE 11	ABOVE 40°	ABOVE 4.4°

If you are living outside
North America, use the chart
to determine your Plant Hardiness Zone.

APPENDIX

METRIC CONVERSIONS

Throughout this book, standard American measures have been used. If you would like to convert the measures to metric measurements, use the following chart as your guide.

Length and distance

Inches x 25.4 = millimeters

Inches x 2.54 = centimeters

Feet x 30.48 = centimeters

Feet x .3048 = meters

Yards x .9144 = meters

Area

Square inches x 6.4516 = cm^2

Square feet x 929.0304 = cm^2

Square feet x .093 = m^2

Square yards x .836 = m^2

SOURCES OF INFORMATION

Garden clubs, horticultural societies, and information service providers, including websites and local agricultural extension agencies, can provide valuable information for gardeners from beginning to advanced. Check your local telephone directory for nearby garden clubs and the county extension office. Following are some websites that offer a range of helpful gardening information.

www.ivillage.com/home/garden

www.neoflora.com

www.gardenweb.com

www.garden-gate.prairienet.org

SOURCES FOR PLANTS AND SUPPLIES

PLANTS

Bear Creek Nursery
P.O. Box 411
Northport, WA 99157
Specializes in cold-hardy fruit trees, shrubs, and berries.

Busse Gardens
13579 10th St. NW
Cokato, MN 55321
(612) 286-2654
Fabulous hardy perennial plants, including wildflowers, hostas, and heucheras.

Comstock Seed
8520 W. 4th St.
Reno, NV 89523
(702) 746-3681
Seed supplier for drought-tolerant native grasses and other plants of the Great Basin.

Edible Landscaping
P.O. Box 77
Afton, VA 22920
(804) 361-9134
Edible for you and the birds and other wildlife—many fruiting trees and shrubs.

Forestfarm
990 Tetherow Road
Williams, OR 97544
(503) 846-7269
Catalog of more than two thousand plants, including Western natives, perennials, and an outstanding variety of trees and shrubs.

The Fragrant Path
P.O. Box 328
Ft. Calhoun, NE 68023
Seeds for fragrant annuals, perennials, shrubs, and vines, many of them old-fashioned favorites.

Gardens of the Blue Ridge
9056 Pittman Gap Road
P.O. Box 10
Pineola, NC 28662
Excellent selection of native trees and shrubs.

Goodwin Creek Gardens
P.O. Box 83
Williams, OR 97544
(541) 846-7375
Specializes in herbs, everlasting flowers, and fragrant plants, as well as plants that attract butterflies and hummingbirds.

Holbrook Farm & Nursery
115 Lance Road
P.O. Box 368
Fletcher, NC 28732
Good selection of flowering shrubs.

Jackson & Perkins
P.O. Box 1028
Medford, OR 97501
(800) 292-4769
Fine selection of roses, perennials, and other garden-worthy plants.

J.L. Hudson, Seedsman
P.O. Box 1058
Redwood City, CA 94064
Seeds, vegetables, herbs, and heirlooms.

Johnny's Selected Seeds
Foss Hill Road
Albion, ME 04910-9731
(207) 437-9294
Grasses, heirlooms, herbs, seeds, supplies, vegetables.

Kurt Bluemel, Inc.
2740 Green Lane
Baldwin, MD 31013
Excellent selection of ornamental grasses, rushes, and sedges.

Lilypons Water Gardens
P.O. Box 10
6800 Lilypons Road
Buckeystown, MD 21717
(301) 874-5133
Plants and supplies for water gardens.

Morden Nurseries, Ltd.
P.O. Box 1270
Morden, MB
Canada R0G 1J0
Wide selection of ornamental trees and shrubs.

Niche Gardens
1111 Dawson Rd.
Chapel Hill, NC 27516
(919) 967-0078
Good, healthy plants of grasses, nursery-propagated wildflowers, perennials, and herbs.

Northwoods Nursery
27368 South Oglesby
Canby, OR 97013
(503) 266-5432
Ornamental trees, shrubs, and vines.

Prairie Moon Nursery
Rt. 3 Box 163
Winona, MN 55987
(507) 452-1362
Generously sized plants and seeds of native prairie grasses and wildflowers.

Prairie Nursery
P.O. Box 306
Westfield, WI 53964
(608) 296-3679
Catalog of prairie grasses and native wildflowers.

Santa Barbara Heirloom
    Seedling Nursery
P.O. Box 4235
Santa Barbara, CA 93140
(805) 968-5444
Organically grown heirloom seedlings of vegetables, herbs, and edible flowers.

Shady Oaks Nursery
112 10th Ave. SE
Waseca, MN 56093
(507) 835-5033
Specializes in plants that thrive in shade, including wildflowers, ferns, perennials, shrubs, and others.

Shepherd's Garden Seeds
30 Irene Street
Torrington, CT 06790
(860) 482-0532
Fine selection of annuals, perennials, vegetables, and herbs.

Southwestern Native Seeds
P.O. Box 50503
Tucson, AZ 85703
Responsibly collected wildflower seeds from the Southwest, West, and Mexico.

Sunlight Gardens
Rt. 1 Box 600-A
Hillvale Rd.
Andersonville, TN 37705
(615) 494-8237
Wonderful selection of wildflowers, all nursery propagated.

Tripple Brook Farm
37 Middle Rd.
Southampton, MA 01073
(413) 527-4626
Wildflowers and other Northeastern native plants, along with fruits and shrubs.

Van Engelen Inc.
23 Tulip Drive
Bantam, CT 06750
Wide variety of bulbs.

Van Ness Water Gardens
2460 N. Euclid Ave.
Upland, CA 91786
(909) 982-2425
Everything you could possibly need for a water garden, from plants to pools to supplies.

Vermont Wildflower Farm
Rt. 7
Charlotte, VT 05445
(802) 425-3500
Excellent wildflower seed and seed mixes.

Wayside Gardens
Garden Lande
Hodges, SC 29695
Offers a wide array of bulbs and perennials.

We-Du Nurseries
Rt. 5 Box 724
Marion, NC 28752
(704) 738-8300
Incredible variety of wildflowers and native perennials from several continents, many woodland plants.

Westgate Garden Nursery
751 Westgate Drive
Eureka, CA 95503
Large selection of rhododendrons and unusual ornamental shrubs and trees.

White Flower Farm
P.O. Box 50
Litchfield, CT 06759
(800) 503-9624
Good selection of plants, including hostas, ferns, and hellebores.

Wildlife Nurseries
P.O. Box 2724
Oshkosh, WI 54903
(414) 231-3780
Plants and seeds of native grasses, annuals, and perennials for wildlife. Also water garden plants and supplies.

Wildwood Gardens
14488 Rock Creek Road
Chardon, OH 44024
Collector's list of dwarf conifers and other dwarf shrubs.

Woodlanders, Inc.
1128 Colleton Ave.
Aiken, SC 29801
(803) 648-7522
Excellent selection of native trees, shrubs, ferns, vines, and perennials, plus other good garden plants.

Yucca Do Nursery
P.O. Box 655
Waller, TX 77484
(409) 826-6363
Good selection of trees, shrubs, and perennial plants, including many natives.

GARDEN ACCENTS

Anderson Design
P.O. Box 4057 C
Bellingham, WA 98227
(800) 947-7697
Arbors, trellises, gates, and pyramids (Oriental, modern, and traditional style).

Bamboo Fencer
31 Germania Street
Jamaica Plain, Boston, MA 02130
(617) 524-6137
Bamboo fences.

Barlow Tyrie Inc.
1263 Glen Avenue Suite 230
Moorestown, NJ 08057-1139
(609) 273-7878
Teak wood garden furniture in English garden style.

Boston Turning Works
42 Plymouth Street
Boston, MA 02118
(617) 482-9085
Distinctive wood finials for gates, fenceposts, and balustrades.

Brooks Barrel Company
P.O. Box 1056
Department GD25
Cambridge, MD 21613-1046
(410) 228-0790
Natural-finish pine wooden barrels and planters.

Charleston Gardens
61 Queen Street
Charleston, SC 29401
(803) 723-0252
Fine garden furnishings.

Doner Design Inc.
Department G
2175 Beaver Valley Pike
New Providence, PA 17560
(717) 786-8891
Handcrafted copper landscape lights.

Florentine Craftsmen Inc.
46–24 28th Street
Department GD
Long Island City, NY 11101
(718) 937-7632
Garden furniture, ornaments, fountains and statuary of lead, stone, and bronze.

Flower Framers by Jay
671 Wilmer Avenue
Cincinnati, Ohio 45226
Flower boxes.

FrenchWyres
P.O. Box 131655
Tyler, TX 75713
(903) 597-8322
Wire garden furnishings: trellis, urns, cachepots, window boxes, arches, and plant stands.

Gardenia
9 Remington Street
Cambridge, MA 02138
(800) 685-8866
Birdhouses.

Gardensheds
651 Millcross Road
Lancaster, PA 17601
Potting sheds, wood boxes, and larger storage units.

Hooks Lattice
7949 Silverton Avenue #903
San Diego, CA 92126
(800) 896-0978
Handcrafted wrought-iron gardenware.

Kenneth Lynch & Sons
84 Danbury ROad
P.O. Box 488
Wilton, CT 06897
(203) 762-8363
Benches, gates, sculpture and statuary, planters and urns, topiary, sundials, and weathervanes.

Kinsman Company
River Road
Department 351
Point Pleasant, PA 18950
(800) 733-4146
European plant supports, pillars, arches trellises, flowerpots, and planters.

Lake Creek Garden Features Inc.
P.O. Box 118
Lake City, IA 51449
(712) 464-8924
Obelisks, plant stands, and gazing globes and stands.

Liteform Designs
P.O. Box 3316
Portland, OR 97208
(503) 253-1210
Garden lighting: path, bullard, accent, step, and tree fixtures.

New Blue Moon Studio
P.O. Box 579
Leavenworth, WA 98826
(509) 548-4754
Trellises, gates, arbors, and garden furniture.

New England Garden
   Ornaments
P.O. Box 235
38 East Brookfield Road
North Brookfield, MA 01535
(508) 867-4474
Garden fountains and statuary, planters and urns, antique furniture, sundials, and limestone ornaments.

Secret Garden
c/o Christine Sibley
15 Waddell Street N.E.
Atlanta, GA 30307
Garden sculpture.

Stone Forest
Department G
P.O. Box 2840
Sante Fe, NM 87504
(505) 986-8883
*Hand-carved granite birdbaths,
basins, fountains, lanterns,
and spheres.*

Sycamore Creek
P.O. Box 16
Ancram, NY 12502
*Handcrafted copper garden
furnishings.*

Tanglewood Conservatories
Silver Spring, MD
*Handcrafted period glass houses
and atriums.*

Tidewater Workshop
Oceanville, NJ 08231
(800) 666-8433
*White cedar benches, chairs,
swings, and tables.*

Toscano
17 East Campbell Street
Department G881
Arlington Heights, IL 60005
(800) 525-1733
*Historic garden sculptures,
including seraphs and cherubs.*

Valcovic Cornell Design
Box 380
Beverly, MA 01915
*Trellises and arbor benches
(traditional to contemporary styles).*

Vixen Hill Manufacturing
    Company
Main Street
Elverson, PA 19520
(800) 423-2766
*Cedar gazebos and screened
garden houses.*

Weatherend Estate Furniture
6 Gordon Drive
Rockland, ME 04841
(800) 456-6483
Heirloom-quality garden furniture.

Wood Classics
Box 96G0410
Gardiner, NY 12525
(914) 255-5651
*Garden benches, swings, chairs
and tables, rockers, lounges,
and umbrellas (all teak and
mahogany outdoor furniture).*

AUSTRALIA

Country Farm Perennials
RSD Laings Road
Nayook VIC 3821

Cox's Nursery
RMB 216 Oaks Road
Thrilmere NSW 2572

Honeysuckle Cottage Nursery
Lot 35 Bowen Mountain Road
Bowen Mountain via Grosevale
NSW 2753

Swan Bros Pty Ltd
490 Galston Road
Dural NSW 2158

CANADA

Corn Hill Nursery Ltd.
RR 5
Petitcodiac NB EOA 2HO

Ferncliff Gardens
SS 1
Mission, British Columbia
V2V 5V6

McFayden Seed Co. Ltd.
Box 1800
Brandon, Manitoba
R7A 6N4

Stirling Perennials
RR 1
Morpeth, Ontario
N0P 1X0

PHOTO CREDITS

©Rob Cardillo: pp. 26, 28 top,
28 bottom, 40 bottom, 50 bottom,
73, 75, 85, 86 top, 95 bottom,
96 top, 107 bottom, 118 top, 135

©David Cavagnaro: pp. 38
bottom, 39 top, 39 bottom,
41 bottom, 49 top, 50 top, 51
bottom, 53 bottom, 97 top, 110,
130, 133

©Todd Davis: pp. 30 bottom,
61 top, 63 top, 63 bottom,
71 bottom, 72 top, 132 bottom

©Brian Durell: pp. 53 top, 97
bottom, 108 bottom

©Tim Elliott: p. 30 top

©Derek Fell: pp. 31, 99, 134 top

The Garden Picture Library:
©Brian Carter: p. 62 top; ©Eric
Crichton: p. 41 top; ©John
Glover: p. 95 top; ©Juliette
Wade: p. 120 top; ©Kit Young:
pp. 96 bottom

©John Glover: p. 2

©Dency Kane: pp. 27 bottom,
38 top, 49 bottom, 82, 83 top,
83 bottom, 84 bottom, 111

©Donna and Tom Krishan: pp.
40 top, 48 top, 48 bottom, 52
top, 60, 71 top, 94 bottom

©Charles Mann: 94 top, 98 top,
134 bottom

©Ken Meyer: pp. 17

©Jerry Pavia: pp. 52 bottom,
119 top, 131, 132 top

©Cheryl Richter: pp. 29, 61
bottom, 62 bottom, 70, 108 top,
119 bottom, 120 bottom, 121
bottom, 122

©Kevin Sheilds: p. 8

©Aleksandra Szywala: pp. 12, 27
top, 72 bottom, 74, 98 bottom,
107 top, 118 bottom

©Mark Turner: pp. 51 top, 106,
109, 121 top

©Rick Wetherbee: pp. 84 top, 86
bottom

INDEX